49572779R00030

GW01451685

The Reader's Megillah

מגילת אסתר

The Book of Esther

Edited by Stephen Games

Published by Gazlet
London and Tel Aviv

GAZLET BOOKS
First paperback edition 2015

Set in Minion Pro Regular 10.5/12.6
and Adobe Hebrew 15/18-19.
Typeset by New Premises Publishing for Gazlet
Printed by CreateSpace, USA

British Library Cataloguing–in–Publication Data:
a catalogue record for this book is available from the British
Library.

ISBN1514790465–978 :13–
ISBN1514790467 :10–

Introduction

The story of *Esther* is an imperfect Biblical text. In this it is not unique. All biblical texts are imperfect, as anyone would expect of documents that have survived long periods of time. Language changes, laws change, cultural attitudes change. It should come as no surprise to find that the same happens to texts, even when one reason for first writing them down rather than committing them to memory was, presumably, to guarantee their integrity.

For some, the fact of textual imperfection has been problematic, especially in recent centuries, with religion under increasing attack, and especially in relation to the Five Books of Moses—the *Chumash*—in which is embodied the *Torah* (the Jewish Law). The Five Books are honoured as the word of God and have been regarded by many as, of necessity, perfect. The *Book of Esther*—*Megillat Esther*—is not, however, a sacred text in the same sense. It was one of the latest additions to the Jewish biblical canon, and was the last to be included in the *Tanakh*, reputedly by the editors referred to collectively as the *Anshei Knesset HaGedolah* (Sages of the Great Assembly) who lived in the period between the end of the Babylonian exile and the start of the Mishnaic period. Set, according to religious scholarship, in the time of Xerxes I, with whom the king in the story, Ahasuerus, is usually identified, the book has traditionally been credited to one or both of the main characters in the story: Mordecai on his own or Mordecai and Esther. This is immediately problematic because Mordecai is spoken of in the third person rather than the first, and described variously as

Esther's cousin and as her adoptive father, in two adjacent but separate passages. In addition the author begins by giving Esther a different name (Hadassah), for reasons that are not explained, and only identifies her real father when referring to him a third time in a later passage.

Greater difficulties than this sit openly and undisguised in the text. The author says of Mordecai that he was 'the son of Jair, the son of Shimei, the son of Kish, a Benjamite, who had been carried away from Jerusalem with the captives that had been carried away with Jeconiah king of Judah, whom Nebuchadnezzar the king of Babylon had carried away'. This cannot be taken at face value because it would have made Mordecai implausibly old at the time of the story because King Jeconiah was among the first to be removed to Babylon following Nebuchadnezzar's conquest of Jerusalem in 597 BCE. There was a second deportation ten years later (587) and a third in 582 but the account suggests that Mordecai was one of the captives carried away with the king rather than subsequently. Jews were allowed to return to Judea in 539, when the Babylonian Empire (strictly speaking the Neo-Babylonian Empire,[1] from 626 BCE) fell to the Achaemenid Persians but many chose to stay and live under Persian rule, and Mordecai was evidently one of them. Babylon's conqueror was Cyrus the Great and Cyrus was succeeded by his son Cambyses II who was succeeded in turn by Darius I. Among Darius's many wives was

---

1   The Neo-Babylonian Empire is usually dated to approx. 626 to 539 BCE.

1

Atossa, a sister of Cambyses, who bore him four sons, one of whom was Xerxes I, Cyrus's grandson, who reigned after Darius's death in 486 BCE. The events in the *Book of Esther* start in the third year of Ahasuerus's reign; Esther becomes a member of the royal household in about the seventh year; and Haman's plot against the Jews begins in the 12th year and is finally foiled in the 13th which, if Ahasuerus is Xerxes, would be about 473 BCE. According to this reckoning, Mordecai has therefore experienced life in pre-exilic Jerusalem, the entirety of the Babylonian captivity and the reigns of two Persian kings before going on to enjoy a productive life as second in command to a third. This would put him well into his second century when the events in Shushan take place. Had Esther been the daughter of his uncle, she would have been over a hundred as well, rather than *'naara y'fat to'ar v'tovat mar'eh'* (a maiden of beautiful form and good to look at). If Ahasuerus is not Xerxes but Cyrus, the very first Persian king after the Babylonians, then Mordecai's chronology is more plausible, but he will have to have been brought to Babylon as a baby to be a minimum age of 60 when the Esther story starts. There is a choice, therefore, between accepting the interior account of Mordecai's life, which makes the externals impossible, and accepting the exterior historicity of Ahasuerus which makes the internals impossible.

An alternative reading is that 'who had been carried away from Jerusalem' refers to the last named—Kish, Mordecai's great-grandfather—and this interpretation helps get round the problem with the timeline. If a generation is measured as being on average 25 years, Mordecai could have been born at any time during the Babylonian capitivity, in which case the timings and text can be reconciled. Treating Kish rather than Mordecai as the captive is not, however, the most natural reading, nor was it the traditional reading until required by the needs of modern literary scholarship and archaeology. Another problem is that 'Kish' is a Babylonian name—indeed, it is the name of a town about 15 miles from the city of Babylon—and it is inconceivable that a pre-exilic Jew would have been given a Babylonian name.

According to the *Book of Esther*, Mordecai lived not in Babylon but in Shushan. Shushan is usually identified with Susa, an ancient Sumerian town dating back to the fifth century BCE that the prophets Daniel and Nehemiah lived in during the Babylonian exile. Susa, 300 kilometres to the east of the city of Babylon and lying between the Dez and Karkheh rivers,[2] became the capital of a small but powerful province called Shushan or Ŝuŝan; late in the third millennium BCE it was taken over by Elamites—in biblical terms the descendants of Elam, the eldest son of Noah's son Shem.

Shushan was important economically, politically and culturally before being sacked by Ashurbanipal in 646 BCE. It then struggled on as a fragmented province until captured between 540–539 by Cyrus who, in recognition of its long and important history, adopted the honorific 'King of Shushan and Anshan' as one of his many titles. Shushan now enjoyed an astonishing revival, with Darius carrying out an extensive programme of civic works, building a new fortress at Susa as his winter residence, promoting the Elamite language as the principal language of the Persian Achaemenid empire and sustaining Elamite deities, cults and priests. The town also became the setting for the earliest surviving play of Aeschylus, *The Persians*, written in 472—the same year in which Haman hatched his plans for the Jews, if Ahasuerus and Xerxes are cognate. The Esther story can even be linked to Susa's Persian renaissance and in this context the description at the start of the book of the luxury of Ahasuerus's palace and lifestyle is not insignificant.

Efforts have been made to identify Mordecai. The name is not Jewish but Aramaic and derives from Marduk,[3] a Mesopotamian god for whom Nebuchadnezzar rebuilt the grand Ésagila temple next to the Etemenanki ziggurat (the inspiration for the Tower of Babel/Babylon). Aramaic ritual texts unearthed between 1936 and 1938 from Persepolis,[4] which was Darius's other main centre of reconstruction, include

2 The Karkheh is said to be another name for Gihon, one of the four rivers serving the Garden of Eden.
3 Egyptian Amun; Greek Zeus.
4 Bowman, R.A., *Aramaic Ritual Texts from Persepolis, Oriental Institute Publications 91*, Chicago: The University of Chicago Press, 1970.

'Marduka' or 'Marduku' among the names of court officials, and this appears to concur with the high status that *Megillat Esther*'s closing verses ascribe to Mordecai. Although at first sight anomalous, the fact of Mordecai's being named after the principal Babylonian deity alerts us only to the pervasiveness of Babylonian culture, to which its Jewish population was no more immune than any others within its sphere of influence. It is even possible that the word 'Marduk' was adopted by Jews in Babylon as a local word for deity, just as English-speaking Jews commonly say 'God' rather than 'Eil' or 'Elohim'. We can suspect this because there is so much other evidence for the transformative effect of Babylon on Jewish experience. Over the course of nearly 60 years, what had been a variant Canaanite culture became an Akkadian culture, losing its Paleo-Hebrew writing in favour of the Aramaic script that Judaism still uses, and adopting Babylonian names for the months.[5] Jewish culture became impregnated with numerous harmless pagan references. Tammuz, the adopted name for the fourth month, for example, was taken from an ancient Akkadian nature god, which no doubt had no more significance than that four of the names of English weekdays derive from Norse gods (Tyr, Odin, Thor and Frigge). That 'Mordecai' probably meant 'a follower or servant of God' also did not make it contentious or heretical. By the same token, it is likely that the name 'Esther' is a variant of 'Ishtar', the Babylonian fertility goddess. The fact that Mordecai and Esther had Babylonian names alerts us also to the likelihood that both were born in Babylon as the children or grandchildren or great-grandchildren of the

5   Before the exile, only four Hebrew months had names: two in the spring (Aviv and Ziv) and two in the autumn (Eithanim and Bul). These became respectively Nissan, Iyar, Tishri and Chesvan. The remaining eight months had previously been known only by their numberical place in the calendar. Thus the fourth month became Tammuz, after an ancient Akkadian nature god, and the fifth month became Av, meaning fiery or hot. It is significant, therefore, that when the Book of Esther says 'In the first month, which is the month Nisan,' or 'in the tenth month, which is the month Tebeth,' it is not being pedantic or repetitive but identfying the month in the Hebrew, then the Babylonian, custom.

Jerusalem captives, rather than their having been taken into captivity themselves. In the case of Mordecai in particular, this calls into question the traditional reading.

The *Megillah* text answers numerous questions concerning the events in the *Esther* story. We learn for example that as a result of their exile from Jerusalem, Jews had dispersed all over the region, to the extent that by the time of Haman's plot, they could be found '*b'chol m'dinot*' ('in all the provinces') of the king. That is to say, they were recent immigrants (albeit unwilling immigrants) to what had been Babylonia and, as we know from the refusal of many to return to Judea, must have adapted well to their new conditions. We can also suppose that unless Haman's plot really was only triggered by what Haman took as Mordecai's discourtesy, the Jews' presence was widely resented. This can be inferred because Mordecai tells Esther not to disclose her Jewish identity to the king before the clash with Haman takes place, and also because Ahasuerus seems at first untroubled by Haman's proposal for the Jews' wholesale slaughter. To be Jewish in the time of Ahasuerus was evidently a handicap.

So far so clear. The story of a plot against the Jews and of the reprisals that ended it can be anchored to a tenable timeline. Admittedly, we no longer have any external corroboration for it: *The Book of the Chronicles* of the kings of Media and Persia, otherwise known as *The Chronicles of King Ahasuerus*, reference to which can be found in *Esther* 2:23, 6:1 and 10:2, and in *Nehemiah* 12:23, has not survived. In spite of that, the coherence of the narrative makes at least a small claim on historicity.

At the same time, even if the story were true and authored by Mordecai, or Mordecai and Esther, rather than by other later hands and rather than being a narrative invention, it has textual imperfections: certain passages break the rules of even the most basic story telling, and the fact that the entire text has remained unchanged for millennia suggests that these imperfections were intrinsic to its history and fundamental to its writing. In Chapter One, for example, the king's feast is referred to first as lasting 180 days and then as lasting seven days. The reader is asked to understand from this that the king gave a second, shorter feast after the first one. Ostensibly this is credible, except that the character of the writing belies such an interpretation. Although magnificent, the first feast is described very briefly (1:3–4), in the manner of an official record. This brevity leaves ambiguities about whom the feast was aimed at, prompting the later addition of three explanatory passages. These inform us that the feast was meant for 'all [the king's] princes and his servants', 'the army of Persia and Media' and 'the nobles and princes of the provinces'. Albeit sequential, these passages cannot be inclusive because of the duplication of 'nobles': they must therefore be variants. The second account (1:5–8) is quite different: it is literary, atmospheric and detailed, and because of the difference in tone, it is best read not as an amplification of the earlier feast or even as an addition to it but as separate, alternative and contradictory.

Conflicting accounts of Ahasuerus's feast in Chapter One of the *Megillah* have no significant bearing on the story. Nor do those at the start of Chapter Eight, where the queen's plea that Ahasuerus annul Haman's decree is introduced in two different ways. In the first (8:3), where we are given only a summary of her actions without hearing the words she speaks, Esther falls at the king's feet and, weeping, begs him '*l'haavir et-roat Haman*'—to 'put away the mischief' that Haman had 'devised against the Jews'. In the longer, second version (8:4–6), we get details, a spoken request, a reminder of what Haman had wanted to do, and a pathetic apostrophe: 'How can I endure to see the evil that shall come unto my people? or how can I endure to see the destruction of my kindred?' We also get in this second version two very similar phrases with variant wording: in addressing the king, Esther says (8:5) 'If it please the king and if I have found favour in his sight' and '[if] the thing seem right before the king and I be pleasing in his eyes'; and in the following line (8:6) 'for how can I endure to see the evil that shall come unto my people?' and 'how can I endure to see the destruction of my kindred?' In both cases, the alternative phrase is a near duplication of the phrase it precedes (and in the standard English translation of the Hebrew, the alternative statement in 8:6 is introduced with 'or'). The

pairing of similar statements is a familiar formula in Hebrew lyric poetry: the *Psalms*—the model for all subsequent lyric prayers—are characterised almost throughout by their antiphonal, call-and-response structure, thus:

> Happy is the man who did not walk in the counsel of the wicked, nor stand in the way of sinners …
> (*Psalms* 1:1)

Esther's duplications may be a conformity to this established poetic model, except that there is no poetic content or ambition anywhere else in the *Megillah* (a topic that will be addressed later in this essay). They read simply as variants.

As stated above, these two examples—in chapters One and Eight—have little impact on the narrative. Other imperfections are more difficult. One example appears in Chapter Five. Here again there are two accounts: the first briefer, the second more expansive and atmospheric. In the first, we learn in just two lines (5:4–5) that after the king asks Esther what she wants, she begs him and Haman to attend her banquet '*hayom*' (today). She obviously wants a favour but seeks to ask it under more auspicious conditions. The king registers this and replies, simply, '*maharu et-Haman laasot et-d'var Esther*' (Make Haman hurry to perform Esther's word), but nothing follows from this instruction and Haman is not hurried to do anything. Instead (in 5:6), the king and Haman appear at the banquet and the king again asks Esther what she wants, rhetorically offering her even half his kingdom. What follows in the standard text is that Esther answers by asking for a second banquet on the following day (in 5:7–8). The king's agreement to this is not stated but is evident from what Haman then tells his wife: that he alone of the king's subjects was invited to today's banquet and alone is invited to tomorrow's. The king's order in respect of Haman has been forgotten. At this point the story is interrupted (in Chapter Six) by the unexpected humiliation of Haman and the rewarding of Mordecai for the latter's having saved the king from an assassination plot (in Chapter Two). Chapter Seven continues with the king and Haman attending the second banquet and the king again asking Esther what she wants, but without Haman giving any sign of the indignity that he has just suffered.

The other most glaring problem in the narrative occurs in the duplication of the revenge brought by the Jews (in Chapter Nine) against those who would have destroyed them, and once again there is a shorter and longer account. The basic story is that with the king's support, the Jews are able to smite all their enemies with the stroke of the sword (9:5), though the help they get from 'the princes of the provinces and the satraps and the governors and they that did the king's business' is credited more to a growing fear of Mordecai, whose power is on the rise, than out of respect for the king. Some 500 men are then reported as having been killed in Shushan fortress on 13th Adar. This is followed by two confused accounts. In the first the king is told that Haman's ten sons, who are named, have been killed. He receives this news and marvels at it. He wonders how many more must have been killed in his other provinces, then offers to fulfil any request by Esther and agrees that the ten sons of Haman should be killed again the next day, 14th Adar.

According to the *Babylonian Talmud* (in Tractate Baba Bathra 15a) the text of the *Book of Esther* was not only included in the canon by the scribes of the Great Assembly but was also redacted by them. What we find odd today (though it seems not to have worried readers in the past) is why those in charge of the text left it in such an unresolved and contradictory state. The answer can only be speculative but we can at least try to see what some of the issues might have been.

In respect of Chapter Five, the problem is one of narrative slippage, where the story-telling is duplicated and the duplications are out of phase with each other. If we take the text literally, we have to suppose that there were two banquets. Perhaps there were. Perhaps the custom of the day was that the greater the favour sought, the greater the number of submissions necessary before the final petition. In purely dramatic terms, however, the first banquet lacks narrative purpose—or at least, none is made explicit—and it is not unreasonable for us to regard this as unsatisfactory, given the self-evident drama of

the rest of the book. People 2,500 years ago may have understood why there was a need for two banquets but we do not, or do not have enough evidence for speculating. At risk of being accused of bringing a modern perspective, we cannot help but be tempted by the view that there was only one banquet and that, as with the feast at the start of the book, we are reading two different descriptions by two different authors. In the first of these, in just three lines (5:4–6), we are given all we need to know about the lead-up to Esther's real petition; in the second version we are given a more elaborate story, set off by a more ingratiating request that the king and Haman attend Esther's banquet the next day.

Except that one version calls for an immediate banquet and the other calls for a delayed banquet, the two passages agree on one thing: there was a banquet. What the second version brings is extra detail that the first version lacks and that all the first of the *Book of Esther*'s paired accounts lack. The second version also adds narrative purpose— and since we have no corroborating evidence, we cannot know whether this is artifice, and therefore an authorial imposition, or a faithful reporting of fact (to the extent that the story has any factual character and that, if so, that character is discernable at all). In the second version, the delaying of Esther's banquet until the next day, or some future day, gives the king enough time to discover Mordecai's virtue and start to doubt Haman's. This prepares the ground for Ahasuerus to agree to Esther's petition, which involves nothing less than her unmasking of herself as Jewish, unmasking the shared fate that she will suffer with her people, and unmasking the king's closest adviser as the greatest threat to her and her people's life.

There is one difficulty in disentangling this part of the story into alternative shorter and longer accounts rather than accepting them as linear and sequential: the fact that Haman himself is 'quoted' as referring to two banquets. As against this, it is only in the shorter account that the king orders 'Cause Haman to make haste' and only in the longer version that chamberlains arrive at Haman's house and hasten him to the banquet. In other words, Haman arrives at the first banquet without having to be hurried and is hurried to the second banquet without the king's having made any such order. This makes no sense. The king's request (in the first version) that Haman hurry to the banquet is only satisfied after Haman has been busily occupied elsewhere (in the second version), parading Mordecai round the town and then returning home and mourning his fate—both of which actions are explicitly performed at speed (Haman has to 'make haste' to carry out the king's will in parading Mordecai, and then has to hurry home to avoid further humiliation and seek his wife's advice). Logically, therefore, line 5:5 should appear in the middle of 6:12:

> 6:12 And Mordecai returned to his king's gate.
> 5:5 Then the king said: 'Cause Haman to make haste, that it may be done as Esther hath said.'
> 6:12 But Haman hasted to his house, mourning and having his head covered.

Not only does this gives dramatic point to Haman's unburdening to Zeresh, it also explains why the king's chamberlains have to fetch Haman and bring him to Esther's banquet, which he now no longer wants to attend. Line 5:5 has evidently become detached from its proper place, so there is good reason to want to challenge the text as we find it. Its relocation also enhances the story's dramatic punch if we regard the story only as literature.

In the case of Chapter Nine, Haman's sons cannot have been killed twice and bright readers can justifiably feel baffled by the duplication and by the failure of the redactors to resolve it.[6] Here, untangling the text does not resolve the problem but may explain why it was left unresolved. What happened in Shushan has to be distinguished from what happened in the other provinces. The Jews in Shushan meted out revenge in the capital on two days—13th and 14th Adar—and rested on the 15th. Jews in the provinces completed their attack on 13th Adar and instituted 14th Adar as their annual day of celebration. To bring the provinces in line with the capital, but also to ensure that the capital respected the provinces, Mordecai instructs the entire Jewish population to keep both days as festivals of celebration: 14th and 15th Adar. The redactors of the Great Assembly were not just secular editors but the representatives of Jewish religious authority. Retaining two conflicting accounts of when the ten sons were hanged may have provided them with the bed of uncertainty needed to persuade the entire Jewish community, wherever it was, to keep a two-day festival.[7]

There is one other possible explanation for the survival of the *Megillah*'s two variant texts and that may have to do with the identity of the authors. Apart from the main body of the text, which is mostly unified, and a couple of places where there seem to be three variations, there are usually only two alternate versions: one that is characteristically briefer and one that is characteristically more detailed and ornamented. This invites us to ask who might have been responsible for each.

Royal courts traditionally sponsored bards or troubadours or dramatists to gather anecdotes and give them epic, lyric or dramatic form. Shakespeare in this sense was a bard to Queen Elizabeth I. As a story emanating from the court of King Ahasuerus, the *Book of Esther* may well have been constructed by one such royal poet (or

---

6 *The New Revised Standard Version of the Bible*, which includes the Greek version of *Esther*, tries to solve the problem of the second hanging by adopting a translation that changes the meaning: '9:13 And Esther said to the king, "Let the Jews be allowed to do the same tomorrow. Also, hang up *the bodies* of Haman's ten sons." 9:14 So he permitted this to be done, and handed over to the Jews of the city the bodies of Haman's sons to hang up.' This suggests that the bodies would be hung up after being massacred, perhaps as a warning, in the way that the decapitated heads of traitors were once put on spikes on London Bridge, but the translator has engaged in supposition and the word 'bodies' does not appear in the Greek. In addition, if the hanging had been meant as a warning rather than a mode of killing, the Hebrew would have specified this.

7 The effort failed, however. Even though the *Megillah* ends with Esther twice confirming Mordecai's instruction, and either Mordecai or the king giving further authority to this religious order, Purim came to be celebrated on one day only: on 15th Adar (known as Shushan Purim) in Jerusalem, in emulation of the custom of Shushan, and—according to the subsequently enacted law—any other city that was walled when Joshua led the people into the Land of Israel; and on 14th Adar everywhere else.

more than one) charged with commemorating the doings of the court, heroising or memorialising its main players, and making events within the royal household available for the wider enjoyment or edification of others, whether nobility or populace.

We know something of how literature of the period was produced in other settings because of the documentation surrounding Aeschylus and *The Persians*, mentioned earlier. *The Persians* is the oldest surviving Greek play and the only surviving Greek tragedy based on contemporary political events. To this extent it is reminiscent of the *Book of Esther*. In almost every other respect it is utterly different. *The Persians* is poetical and dramatic, highly stylised, full of Aeschylus's difficult language, and designed to be partly spoken and partly sung. It is populated by two main characters (King Darius and his royal mother), a messenger, a ghost (Xerxes) and a chorus of elders). Its deliberate contrivance—what makes it almost impossible to perform today—is partly what won Aeschylus first prize at the Dionysia festival in Athens in 472 BCE. The *Book of Esther*, by contrast, appears to have been written in simple demotic Hebrew. It is easy to understand, familiar in its vocabulary and lacking in structural complexity (unless its narrative oddities are an attempt at sophistication). It is as accessible as the popular entertainments of Yiddish theatre a century ago. This is noteworthy in view of the trend in literature for poetry—an earlier literary form—to give way to prose as literacy becomes more widespread. *Esther*, in common with many other books in the Bible, is surprisingly prosaic, suggesting that literacy was long established within the culture from which it sprang.

There is another curiosity here. The *Megillah* is not the only version of the *Book of Esther*. There are also two Greek versions, a longer Beta-text that appeared in the Greek translation of the Bible (the Septuagint) and a shorter Alpha-text, also known as the Lucianic recension. These contain the 'Jewish' text but with six quite extensive additions as well as many small but significant textual changes. The first main addition is a prologue to the story in which Mordecai, described as a great man already

serving in the king's court, has a dream. In the dream he hears thunder and explosions and sees two huge roaring dragons preparing to fight, as well as the nations of the world preparing to join battle to subdue 'the righteous nation'. The righteous nation is terrified and cries out to God, after which it is delivered by sunlight pouring from a tiny spring that becomes a great river. Mordecai wakes and tries to make sense of what he takes to be a portent of God's will. The prologue is matched by an epilogue in which Mordecai interprets what he now sees as the fulfilment of that portent: the spring that became a river is Esther, the two dragons are Haman and himself, the nations are those who would have destroyed the Jews, and the righteous nation is Israel.

These additions are intriguing because they recall the folk culture of Babylon and Persian neo-Babylon, which was rife with legends about fairies, monsters and demons. These ranged, over the course of more than 1,500 years of Akkadian literature, from ancient epics such as the creation myth *Enûma Eliš*, about the victory of Marduk over the water-chaos dragon Tiamat, to later prophetic texts, incantations, histories, myths, fables and comedies. A surprising amount of this has survived, at least in fragments, and some of the best examples occur in stories written or revised by and for the Jewish community in Babylon. Some of these are canonical: the second Jewish creation myth in *Genesis* (magic serpent persuades Eve to commit the first sin) and the *Book of Jonah* (recalcitrant prophet gets eaten and then vomited by giant fish).[8] The rest are Jewish demon writings that were preserved by being translated into Greek (whether from Hebrew or Aramaic originals) and incorporated into the Septuagint but not included in the

8 Among other canonical examples, apart from references to the idols of other nations, are the teraphim and nephilim (in *Genesis*); the destroyer (in *Exodus* and elsewhere); the kherubim (in *Exodus*); Balaam's talking donkey (in *Numbers*); the four winged creatures (in Ezekiel); the behemoth and leviathan (in Job); the four allegorical monsters (the lion with an eagle's wings, the bear-like creature, the leopard with four wings and four heads, and the creature with iron teeth and ten horns) that come out of the sea and threaten the world (in *Daniel*); and angels (various).

Jewish canon—hence 'deuterocanonical'—such as *Bel and the Dragon*[9] (Daniel kills a Babylonian dragon-deity by feeding it *matzot*—barley cakes—that cause it to explode when eaten) and the *Book of Tobit* (angel helps son of a man blinded by bird droppings to use the entrails of a fish that tries to swallow him (a) to drive away a demon that has so far killed seven men before they can consummate their marriage to the woman he wishes to marry, and (b) to cure his father's blindness).

Apart from the story of Eve and the serpent and the *Book of Jonah*, Jewish redactors did not like demon stories even though such stories might include within them affirmations of the greater power and virtue of God. In the first part of *Bel and the Dragon*, for example, Daniel proves that an idol (Bel) worshiped by King Cyrus is a false deity and goes on to kill a dragon, for which he is thrown into a lions' den (as before, in the *Book of Daniel* Chapter 6) but is saved by a prophet, causing the king to proclaim 'Great art thou, O Lord God of Daniel, and there is none other besides thee.' In *Tobit*, the blinded Tobit prays to God for death; before their first wedding night, his son and daughter-in-law pray to God for life; and when they all meet and Tobit's sight is restored they all give thanks to God. Similarly, in the Greek version of *Esther*, after 4:17 in the *Megillah*, when Haman's plot is revealed, first Mordecai prays to God at length, then Esther prays to God at even greater length, and both use formulas of supplication still employed in Jewish prayer today. The Greek text has numerous other references to God as an active force in the world, in stark contrast to the Jewish *Megillah*, in which God goes unmentioned.

According to tradition, translation of Judaism's canonical texts into Greek began in the early third century BCE on the orders of the Egyptian king, Ptolemy II Philadelphus, and was complete by the late second century BCE. Tradition also holds that the translation of the fundamental texts—the Five Books of Moses—was strikingly rigorous and consistent while translation of the later texts was more wayward. In respect of how the story of Esther was formalised, we may assume that there was a certain amount of interplay between the Jewish redactors and their Greek counterparts. At the same time, those who formalised Judaism's canonical texts are customarily said to have exercised tight editorial control: they had access to the Greek additions but they excluded them. In the case of *Esther*, they had the option of re-writing the Esther story as a religious morality tale using their own or other, non-Greek material and chose not to. Thus, although the *Megillah* ends by quoting Mordecai's call for a two-day festival in recognition of the Jews' salvation, the Jewish version is explicitly historical and temporal.

There are two possible reasons. First, *Esther* ends with the statement that 'the history of the king's power and strength, and the account of the greatness of Mordecai, whom the king promoted, are recorded in the *Book of Chronicles* of the kings of Media and Persia.' Judaism had its own *Book of Chronicles* (*Divrei HaYamim*) which provides a history of the biblical southern kingdom (Judea), focusing on the role of Jerusalem as Judaism's pre-exilic religious centre and largely ignoring Jewish life as it was lived in Egypt, the wilderness, the northern kingdom (Israel), Nineveh and Babylon. It ends with Cyrus inviting the Jewish people to return to Jerusalem and licensing the rebuilding of the Temple (completed under Darius). The later story of Esther is therefore outside its timespan and editorial remit; it follows that its origins must lie elsewhere.

Since *Esther* refers twice to the *Book of Chronicles* of the kings of Media and Persia, now lost, it is fair to assume that the text as we have it may have been taken over verbatim or largely verbatim from here instead. That is to say, although it records a Jewish victory, *Esther* may not in its origins be a Jewish but a Persian story, with no editorial or religious agenda except as the record of an affair of state. If this is so, the Jewish editors imported into the scriptural canon an authentic external document—a court manuscript—and were scrupulous in not ascribing or adding to it religious content that it, as a Persian text, was not competent to provide.

There is a second and equally plausible explanation for the absence of religious

9   The story appears as Chapter 14 in the extended Greek version of the *Book of Daniel*.

references in *Esther*. When God appears as a presence in other Neo-Babylonian biblical works, he acts to balance the malign force of other magical creatures that intervene in the world. To this extent his status is diminished: he may be the most powerful and kindly of these other-worldy entities but he is not unique. This is essentially the theology of Zoroastrianism, the religion inspired by the sixth-century BCE Persian mystic Zoroaster (Zarathustra), with whom all the principal Persian rulers of Babylon are thought to have been personally and formally associated. Zoroastrianism posited a single, beneficent and ultimately omnipotent god, Ahura Mazdā,[10] constantly preoccupied with having to suppress evil spirits that provoked and tried to undermine him.

Zoroastrian belief can be seen as a projection of Persia's politics: the endless struggles of Cyrus, Cambyses, Darius and Xerxes to keep down other nations—Egyptians, Greeks, Medes, Babylonians, etc—as well as internal rebels. This was a template that Babylonian Jews, displaced from their land and untroubled by imperial ambition, had no reason to share. Since 597 BCE, their politics had been a matter solely of self-management; as a nation in exile they were at the mercy of their captors. Unlike the Persians, the Jewish template was therefore one of total dependency on a higher power, whether temporal or spiritual. This is important in how the Jewish view of God developed and diverged from the religious views of politically more autonomous neighbours.

Political circumstances further complicated Jewish thinking. Magical relativism was imprinted into Babylonian culture: ungovernable occult forces were a constant threat and human beings had no choice but to try and placate them. To this chaos of fear, the Persians brought a less terrifying idea: that of stratified discord. Within Zoroastrianism, Ahura Mazdā occupies a higher realm; evil spirits—the minions of the evil Angra Mainyu or Ahriman—occupy a lower one; and the two sides play out their conflicts in the earthly middleground where human beings live. Humans get involuntarily caught up in their battles, either directly or as part of the collateral damage, but need only focus their efforts on propitiating the one higher god.

In spite of their Zoroastrianism, the Achaemenid rulers that the Jews lived under all adopted a policy of religious pluralism: from Cyrus to Xerxes, conquered people were allowed and even encouraged to worship their own gods. This tolerance dampened dissent and made possible the social stability that powered Neo-Babylon's massive economic renaissance. Babylon's Jews benefited greatly but also knew that the policy of tolerance could be reversed at any moment and by no means had the assent of Babyon's indigenous elite or, in particular, its priestly class—*pro tem* less powerful than formerly but always looking for an opportunity to rise again. As captives, the Jews had nowhere to escape to and, unlike other nations, no access to military force, which is what makes the conclusion of the *Esther* story so distinct. They were, moreover, easily identifiable as religious non-conformists: in this respect, Mordecai is acutely aware of Esther's vulnerability, and of his own, and of the people's. As Haman says to Ahasuerus (3:8): 'There is a certain people scattered abroad and dispersed among the peoples in all the provinces of thy kingdom and their laws are diverse from those of every people, neither keep they the king's laws. Therefore it profiteth not the king to suffer them.'

The Jews' best interest lay, therefore, in keeping a low profile, which meant overt obedience to the king, even at risk of offending the local upper classes (as Mordecai offended Haman). Any perception of divided loyalty had to be resisted. The absence of God in the *Book of Esther* is thus an illustration of a strategic silence. In this narrative, the highest force in the land is the king and everything that happens is the product of his assent. It is Ahasuerus who has to be propitiated, first by Haman who offers to put ten thousand talents of silver into the king's treasuries, and then more powerfully by Esther who fasts for three days, hosts a banquet (or two banquets), employs her charisma and beauty, weeps and entreats, calls on the king's powers—his legal mechanisms, royal scribes, fast messengers, and horses from the royal stud—to reinforce his

10   Also known as Ormizd and Ormazd.

authority, and organises a blood bath in the king's name to prove his military might.

The most patent explanation for the mostly secular character of *Esther* is, finally, that it records the Jews' victory over Haman as a direct consequence of 'the king's commandment and his decree' and of no other agency (other than Mordecai's promptings and Esther's machinations). In that sense, the *Megillah* is a tribute or testimonial to the temporal power. This is what the king in question would have demanded, what anyone reading the story would have expected, and what anyone associated with the court and attentive to his or her own survival would have set out to write. Since the book makes reference to scribes several times, it is possible that scribes—those referred to or others—were involved in its production, either directly and creatively or in a merely secretarial capacity. Jewish tradition takes no position on this. Tradition suggests, however, as already noted, that the book was written by Mordecai on his own or by Mordecai and Esther. In the absence of evidence it is impossible to comment on this with confidence but the presence of two alternative versions of the story, as discussed above, does suggest dual authorship. The tone of the two voices has already been referred to: the first brief and unornamented, the second more detailed and florid. More significantly, the second voice tends to contain inside information more likely to have been known to Esther, or an Esther character, than to Mordecai, or a Mordechai character: details of the housing and grooming of virgins for the king's pleasure in Chapter Two, of other events that took place in the king's palace to which a Mordecai would not have been privy, of the wording of conversations with Hathach (Chapter Four) and Ahasuerus (Chapter Five *et seq*), and of the take-up of the king's revised edict in the provinces rather than just in Shushan (Chapter Nine). In the same way, the more perfunctory versions suggest less first-hand knowledge.

For convenience, therefore, though this is only fanciful, we have labelled the two versions 'Mordecai' and 'Esther' or M and E.

The M text is more concerned with authority, reputation and the excellence of majesty, and where there is a choice it is always the M text that appears first. It is M that announces the scope of Ahasuerus's reign, the monumentality of his half-year feast, and the nobility and military prowess of those who attended the feast and whose entry into the city would have been marked by ceremonial honours. It is M that provides information about Esther, gives credence to her exceptional allure, and concentrates on those of her actions that have a decisive effect. The E text invariably follows, providing background and colour, and in 8:5–6 introducing the *Megillah*'s only moment of poetry. We might regard M here as representative of the more objective historiography of emergent Athenian culture, Thucydidean in its detachment and ambition, and E as representative of an older, more subjective Persian tradition of storytelling.

In some parts of the *Megillah* the story is carried not by two texts but by one. Some readers may regard these solo passages as detached from the M/E polarity or even as evidence of its absence or non-existence; others may read them as essentially M or essentially E. It is the view of this essay that each may indeed be either M or E, but that without more information, it is impossible to say which of the two they are. The long-winded account of how the king's second decree was published in the provinces (8:9–14) repeats the same literary formula that was used to recall the publishing of the first decree (3:12–15), including the same repetitive tripartite structure. This detail and repetition may reflect the conventional flourishes of formal records or the garrulousness or officiousness of the reporter. To choose one interpretation rather than another, however, let alone ascribing garrulousness to E and officiousness to M, is unsafe and means resorting to stereotypes—gender stereotypes and literary stereotypes.

In some passages, for example, we may think we hear overtones of a Polonius. When Mordecai is reported as putting on sackcloth and coming to the king's gate (4:2), a caveat is attached, explaining that Mordecai does not go beyond the king's gate because 'none might enter within the king's gate clothed in sackcloth'. This can be read as the writings of a court bureaucrat for whom etiquette is all important. Similarly, the way in which Ahasuerus's ignorance of Esther's origins is framed—that Esther had 'not yet made known her kindred nor her people, as Mordecai had charged her' (2:20)—can be read not just as a neutral piece of information about what the king knew but as a comment on Esther's deference and obedience to Mordecai. Both texts are in that sense self-serving: the first remark (on etiquette) is self-excusing and a little pompous, the second remark (on Esther) is a compliment on the control that Mordecai still exercises over the young queen. If this second remark is an M text, it functions as a condescending observation on Esther's compliance as Mordecai's still dutiful step-daughter, but it is not necessarily this. The examples might just as well be by Esther, or an Esther-type scribe, in the first case priding herself on an awareness of court protocols and in the second case confirming the queen's (or the writer's) sense of discretion. In short, without a balancing text, we cannot tell whether these solo, uncontested examples are written from a female or male perspective, or by an ingenue or a court habitué. The first example may indicate a girlish nervousness about protocol; the second may reveal Esther's (or an E's) rather than Mordecai's (or an M's) pride in the queen's piety. Nor is there evidence that these are even the writings of a younger or older person. That the story is about a young Esther does not means that a young Esther, or a young E, wrote it. The portrait of Esther is what one would expect of a literary composition and may be the contrivance of an Esther when older or of a more experienced third party.

With this warning in mind, we have to work very hard to resist the interpretation of Polonian pettiness. At the start of Chapter Nine, for example, we might consider that the narrative is interrupted twice and then delayed twice for no reason except pedantry. The basic sentence runs as follows:

> 9:1 Now in the twelfth month which is the month Adar on the thirteenth day of the same when the king's command and his decree drew near to be put in execution, 9:2 the Jews gathered together in their cities throughout all the provinces of King Ahasuerus to lay hand on such as sought their hurt,

and no man could withstand them for the fear of them was fallen upon all the peoples.

Although straightforward, this sentence is broken into twice just before 9:2, first with this:

> in the day that the enemies of the Jews hoped to have rule over them

and then by this:

> whereas it was turned to the contrary that the Jews had rule over them that hated them.

The two additions are redundant: instead of driving the drama forwards, they slow it down; and in any case we already have these facts. The action is then held up further by no less than three character references. All we need to know is what line 9:5 says:

> 9:5 And the Jews smote all their enemies with the stroke of the sword and with slaughter and destruction and did what they would unto them that hated them.

Instead, we have to wait for:

> 9:3 And all the princes of the provinces and the satraps and the governors and they that did the king's business helped the Jews because the fear of Mordecai was fallen upon them

and:

> 9:4 For Mordecai was great in the king's house and his fame went forth throughout all the provinces,

and:

> for the man Mordecai waxed greater and greater.

We might be forgiven for reading into at least two of these additions an M voice that gets louder from 9:20. From here to the end of the *Megillah*, it is Mordecai who attracts all the attention—as the king's Number Two, the Jews' Number One and no longer the queen's step-father but her joint-equal father:

9:29 Then wrote Queen Esther *the daughter of* [Abihail and of] *Mordecai the Jew.*

It is Mordecai who now takes on Ahasuerus's job of sending out orders to the provinces, apparently without reference upwards, almost overshadowing the king in his zeal and new-found importance. Lest he put himself at risk, Mordecai tactically acknowledges (10:3) that he was 'second unto King Ahasuerus' but then basks in the fact that he too is now memorialised alongside the king in the imperial *Book of Chronicles* and that he is adored by his people. Both within the events of the story and the structure of the language, Mordecai completely displaces the book's eponymous heroine.

We might here be forgiven for discerning a tension, even a competitiveness, between Mordecai and Esther in the way that the story oscillates between M passages and E passages (if this is how we choose to read them). In Chapter Nine, the account of events in Shushan where Mordecai is now in effective control seems to be carried by M texts that favour Mordecai but is interrupted by E texts that stress what is happening further afield, and do so in a way that seems to challenge Mordecai's monopoly. An M text at 9:15, for example, talks about the killings in Shushan on 14th Adar; an E text at 9:16 then ignores this information and talks about the killings in the provinces the day before. Similarly, an M text at 9.18 stresses that the Jews in Shushan rampaged for two days and celebrated on the third while an E text at 9:19 determines that provincial Jews rampaged for only one day and celebrated on the second.

This putative contest between M texts and E texts is not just a matter of arguing about who dictates the public record: it is personal as well. At 8:3, an M text writes off Esther's pleas to the king as girlish weeping until a lengthier E text at 8:4–6 counters by quoting the psalmic lyricism of what she actually said. Similarly, the implied sequitur that 'The Jews smote all their enemies with the stroke of the sword' (9:5) because 'Mordecai was great in the king's house' (9:4) is contradicted at 9:13 by an E text that attributes the killings in Shushan not to Mordecai's power but to Esther's entreaties. More pointedly, the M text at 9.4 ('For Mordecai was great in the king's house and his fame went forth throughout all the provinces') appears to be challenged by the altogether more ambivalent E text substitution: 'for the man Mordecai waxed greater and greater'—'the man', not 'the king's new deputy'.

In literary terms, the E texts deploy the theme of reversal against the theme of celebrity. In an M text at 9:20, Mordecai is credited with converting local one-day Purim celebrations into an empire-wide two-day event—a clever political initiative meant to knit Shushanite and provincial Jews together—but in a corresponding E text (9:25), the main credit is shifted to Esther for having persuaded the king to reverse Haman's plan. In the same way, one of the interruptions at the start of Chapter Nine ('whereas it was turned to the contrary that the Jews had rule over them that hated them') reminds the reader of Esther's role, not Mordecai's, in reversing Ahasuerus's decision and bringing matters to a happy conclusion.

The object of this exercise has not been to determine whether the Esther story is a real historical event or a folktale, as many scholars now hold it to be. In the absence of definitive evidence, it might be either or a mixture of both. For the purposes of this study, the rootedness of the story in reality or fable is immaterial; what matters here is how the narrative was constructed and what function it performed, and that requires an understanding of the techniques of literary criticism. For example, the language used to describe Mordecai in the ninth and tenth chapters has conventionally been thought of as respectful, as befitting a heroic leader who saw an opportunity and a threat, took appropriate action in both cases and had the gratification of seeing both his interventions succeed, to his own and his people's considerable advantage. If we take this view, the idea of rival M texts and E texts, of competition between Esther and Mordecai, and of the narrative as nuanced and coded has to be dismissed—but that also means choosing not to see what is in front of us. To treat the text as editorially neutral—even to treat it as hagiographic or heroising—is to blind oneself to what actually appears.

Even if one ignores the new interpretations that literary analysis offers, we are still left with sufficient evidence of variant texts, repetitions, inconsistencies, changes of emphasis and stylistic alternatives to reveal the book not as a seamless work but a patchwork quilt. We know as a matter of historic record, in any case, that additional material—the Greek additions and changes— were excluded from the canonic text and we can now speculate on why. Much of the Greek material seems to have been offered up in order to give the *Megillah* the religious dimension that it otherwise lacks. This was evidently not welcome to the editors, for two reasons at least. One has already been discussed: the wish to preserve the secularity of the story as a homage to the ruling powers. The other relates to the source. From the period when the events in *Esther* appear to have taken place to the period when the story was redacted, the Persian empire was troubled by various Greek city states that were also at war with each other. Cyrus had conquered the region of Ionia in 547. Persian rule led in 499 to an Ionian revolt that, though not without some success—notably the destruction of the Persian capital at Sardis—was finally put down in 493. Darius then sent two invasionary forces to conquer Greece, the first in 492 only partially successful, the second in 490 ending in Persian defeat by the Athenians at the Battle of Marathon. In retaliation, Xerxes launched a second invasion in 480 that succeeded on land but was routed at sea. Persian ambitions were finally denied in 479 when the Greeks destroyed both the Persian army and its fleet, and by extension ensured the rise of what is now regarded as a more purely Greek culture and a western civilisation based on Greek rather than Persian or Perso-Greek foundations. The Persians continued to be driven back during the 470s and hostilities were finally brought to an end, apparently by treaty, around 449.

It is self-evident that there was much at stake in relations between Persians and Greeks. It is also evident that while much of the Jewish world lived in areas under Greek rule or Greek influence, Jewish authority continued to operate from a base that was under Persian control. According to Jewish tradition, the Great Assembly, if it ever existed as an entity (which is now doubted), was instituted by Ezra and centred on Jerusalem after Cyrus gave the Jews of Babylon freedom to return to Judea. The Assembly, or the authority of its supposed 120 sages, spanned several centuries and among its earliest members was Zerubabel (meaning 'born in Babylon'),[11] the grandson of Jehoiachin, the penultimate king of Judah, and the man credited with leading the first Jews back to Jerusalem.[12] Zerubabel was appointed first governor of Judea under Persian rule by Darius and completed the rebuilding of the Temple that Cyrus had sanctioned. Judea remained a Persian province for two hundred years, from 539 to 332, when it was taken over by the Macedonian Greeks under Alexander. In all that time, the religious and political authorities in Jerusalem were aware that their continued existence in Judea was on sufferance and that just as the Jews had been allowed to return by the Persians, they could also be transported back to Babylon again at any time. We therefore have to read a measure of political caution into all writings of this period. While it is clear that a substantial proportion of Persia's Jewish population had already become hellenised long before Judea became a Greek client state, the authorities in Jerusalem had a vested interest in not favouring Greek ideas if there was any risk that by doing so they might destabilise their own status quo. This must go some way to explaining the reluctance to include Greek materials in the Jewish canon.

The issues discussed above are represented visually in the pages that follow by means of a layout that separates the different putative authorial voices into separate columns. The reader should note that all the sentences (*pesukim*) are numbered sequentially in accordance with the standard text. By following the number at the start of each *pasuk*, it is possible to follow the Megillah in its conventional form, though this will not infrequently involve darting back and

11 The name is traditionally spelled Zerubbabel in English but there is no etymological reason for the second b.
12 Mordecai is also said to have been among those who returned to Jerusalem, but nothing in the final verses of *Esther* supports this.

forth from one side of the page to the other. If, however, one reads down one or other of the two main columns one starts to hear with clarity the distinct tone of each of the two voices referred to above: the M voice (in the column adjacent to the gutter of the double page) and the E voice (in the outer column).

For convenience, the two columns have been separated by vertical rules. In a handful of cases the columns are further sub-divided. This is meant to show where additional information seems to have been interpolated, (a) to add extra detail or (b) to reinforce what had already been said (often resulting in unhelpful redundancy) or (c) out of editorial deference to the speaker, all presumably after the main text was established. More often than not, however, there is porosity between the columns where the story flips from one speaker to the other or where one speaker interjects with an alternative report. Where this is the case, the vertical rule is broken to allow the reader's gaze to slip sideways to discover the nature of the interruption. Towards the end of Chapter 9, however, the two voices are so insistently separate that the rule has been left unbroken. The reader must decide whether such a decision is warranted.

In general, passages that start on the same line but in different columns should be regarded as alternates and therefore equal in importance. Commentaries and amplifications that appear in sub-divided columns should be regarded as subsidiary or secondary to the main narrative thrust. Where the narrative is uncontested, it crosses the full page.

It is my hope that readers will find this edition of the Megillah helpful in revealing self-evident duplications, redundancies and narrative contradictions. A key to the most telling divergences appears in the Notes at the end of the book.

Several people have kindly given me advice and feedback during the writing of this study. In particular I wish to thank Aaron J. Koller, Willem Smelik, Stephen Massil and Robin Stamler for the very enjoyable correspondence that we have exchanged while the work was in preparation, and Raphaël Freeman and Zaki Elia for their thoughts on my typography. I also wish to thank my wife, Bracha (Bea) Games née Nemeth for first stoking my interest in the *Megillah*, following her own lead in learning the trope.

Stephen Games
Muswell Hill 2015 / 5775–6

The Reader's Megillah

מגילת אסתר

The Book of Esther: Megillat Esther
Chapter 1

M	E

M

1 Now it came to pass in the days of Ahasuerus

> (this is Ahasuerus who reigned from India to Ethiopia over a hundred and twenty seven provinces)

3 in the third year of his reign he made a party for

all his princes and his servants,	the army of Persia and Media,	the nobles and princes of the provinces

being before him,

4 when he showed the riches of his glorious kingdom and the honour of his excellent majesty many days even a hundred and fourscore days. 5 And when these days were fulfilled

9 Vashti the queen also made a party for the women in the royal house of King Ahasuerus.

E

2 In those days when King Ahasuerus sat on the throne of his kingdom

> (which was in Shushan fortress)

the king made for all the people, great and small, that were in Shushan fortress a seven-day party in the court of the garden of the king's quarters. 6 There were hangings of white green and blue bordered by cords of linen and purple wool on rods of silver and pillars of marble. The couches were of gold and silver on a paved floor of green and white and shell and onyx marble. 7 Drinks were served in cups of gold, the cups being of various designs, with royal wine aplenty by the king's bounty. 8 And the drinking was according to the law: none did compel for so the king had ordered all the servants of his house that they should do exactly according to every man's pleasure. [S]

10 On the seventh day

[W]hen the heart of the king was merry with wine he commanded Mehuman, Bizzetha, Harbona, Bigtha and Abagtha, Zethar and Carcas, the seven chamberlains that officiated in the presence of Ahasuerus the king, 11 to bring Queen Vashti before the king

> wearing the royal crown

to show the peoples and the princes her beauty, for she was fair to look on.

12 But Queen Vashti refused to come at the king's commandment that the chamberlains had handed her, so the king was furious and his anger burned in him. [S]

13 Then the king said to the wise men who knew astrology

מְגִלַּת אֶסְתֵּר
פֶּרֶק א

<table>
<tr><td>E</td><td>M</td></tr>
</table>

M

א וַיְהִי בִּימֵי אֲחַשְׁוֵרוֹשׁ

הוּא אֲחַשְׁוֵרוֹשׁ
הַמֹּלֵךְ מֵהֹדּוּ וְעַד־כּוּשׁ
שֶׁבַע וְעֶשְׂרִים וּמֵאָה
מְדִינָה.

ג בִּשְׁנַת שָׁלוֹשׁ לְמָלְכוֹ עָשָׂה מִשְׁתֶּה לְ-

| כָּל־שָׂרָיו | חֵיל פָּרַס | הַפַּרְתְּמִים וְשָׂרֵי |
| וַעֲבָדָיו | וּמָדַי | הַמְּדִינוֹת |

לְפָנָיו.

ד בְּהַרְאֹתוֹ אֶת־עֹשֶׁר כְּבוֹד מַלְכוּתוֹ וְאֶת־יְקָר תִּפְאֶרֶת גְּדוּלָתוֹ יָמִים רַבִּים שְׁמוֹנִים וּמְאַת יוֹם. ה וּבִמְלוֹאת הַיָּמִים הָאֵלֶּה

E

ב בַּיָּמִים הָהֵם כְּשֶׁבֶת הַמֶּלֶךְ אֲחַשְׁוֵרוֹשׁ עַל כִּסֵּא מַלְכוּתוֹ

אֲשֶׁר בְּשׁוּשַׁן הַבִּירָה.

עָשָׂה הַמֶּלֶךְ לְכָל־הָעָם הַנִּמְצְאִים בְּשׁוּשַׁן הַבִּירָה לְמִגָּדוֹל וְעַד־קָטָן מִשְׁתֶּה שִׁבְעַת יָמִים בַּחֲצַר גִּנַּת בִּיתַן הַמֶּלֶךְ. ו חוּר כַּרְפַּס וּתְכֵלֶת אָחוּז בְּחַבְלֵי־בוּץ וְאַרְגָּמָן עַל־גְּלִילֵי כֶסֶף וְעַמּוּדֵי שֵׁשׁ מִטּוֹת זָהָב וָכֶסֶף עַל רִצְפַּת בַּהַט־וָשֵׁשׁ וְדַר וְסֹחָרֶת. ז וְהַשְׁקוֹת בִּכְלֵי זָהָב וְכֵלִים מִכֵּלִים שׁוֹנִים וְיֵין מַלְכוּת רָב כְּיַד הַמֶּלֶךְ. ח וְהַשְּׁתִיָּה כַדָּת אֵין אֹנֵס כִּי־כֵן יִסַּד הַמֶּלֶךְ עַל כָּל־רַב בֵּיתוֹ לַעֲשׂוֹת כִּרְצוֹן אִישׁ־וָאִישׁ. [ס]

ט גַּם וַשְׁתִּי הַמַּלְכָּה עָשְׂתָה מִשְׁתֵּה נָשִׁים בֵּית הַמַּלְכוּת אֲשֶׁר לַמֶּלֶךְ אֲחַשְׁוֵרוֹשׁ.

י בַּיּוֹם הַשְּׁבִיעִי

כְּטוֹב לֵב־הַמֶּלֶךְ בַּיָּיִן אָמַר לִמְהוּמָן בִּזְּתָא חַרְבוֹנָא בִּגְתָא וַאֲבַגְתָא זֵתַר וְכַרְכַּס שִׁבְעַת הַסָּרִיסִים הַמְשָׁרְתִים אֶת־פְּנֵי הַמֶּלֶךְ אֲחַשְׁוֵרוֹשׁ. יא לְהָבִיא אֶת־וַשְׁתִּי הַמַּלְכָּה לִפְנֵי הַמֶּלֶךְ

בְּכֶתֶר מַלְכוּת

לְהַרְאוֹת הָעַמִּים וְהַשָּׂרִים אֶת־יָפְיָהּ כִּי־טוֹבַת מַרְאֶה הִיא.

יב וַתְּמָאֵן הַמַּלְכָּה וַשְׁתִּי לָבוֹא בִּדְבַר הַמֶּלֶךְ אֲשֶׁר בְּיַד הַסָּרִיסִים וַיִּקְצֹף הַמֶּלֶךְ מְאֹד וַחֲמָתוֹ בָּעֲרָה בוֹ. [ס]

יג וַיֹּאמֶר הַמֶּלֶךְ לַחֲכָמִים יֹדְעֵי הָעִתִּים

(for this was the king's
way [to ask] all who
knew law and judging)

14 (and those closest to
him were Carshena,
Shethar, Admatha,
Tarshish, Meres,
Marsena and Memucan,
the seven princes of
Persia and Media who
saw the king's face and
sat in highest rank in
the kingdom)

15 'What by law can be done unto Queen Vashti since she has not carried out
the request of King Ahasuerus as sent by the chamberlains?' [S]

16 And Memucan answered before the king and the princes: 'Vashti the queen hath not done wrong
to the king only but also to all the princes and to all the peoples that are in all the provinces of the king
Ahasuerus. 17 For this deed of the queen will be revealed unto all women and make their husbands
contemptible in their eyes when it will be said: 'The King Ahasuerus commanded Vashti the queen to
be brought in before him but she came not.' 18 And this day will the princesses of Persia and Media
who have heard of the deed of the queen say the like unto all the king's princes. So will there arise
enough contempt and wrath. 19 If it please the king, let there go forth a royal commandment from
him and let it be written among the laws of the Persians and the Medes that it be not altered that
Vashti come no more before King Ahasuerus and that the king give her royal estate unto another that
is better than she. 20 And when the king's decree which he shall make shall be published throughout
all his kingdom, great though it be, all the wives will give to their husbands honour both to great and
small.' 21 And the word pleased the king and the princes, and the king did according to the word of
Memucan 22 for he sent letters

into all the king's provinces | into every province

according to the writing thereof and to every people after their language that every man should
bear rule in his own house and speak according to the language of his people. [S]

Chapter 2

1 After these things when the wrath of King Ahasuerus had subsided he remembered Vashti and what
she had done and what was decreed against her. 2 Then said the king's servants who ministered to him:
'Let there be sought for the king young virgins fair to look on 3 and let the king appoint officers in all
the provinces of his kingdom that they may gather together all the fair young virgins unto Shushan
fortress to the house of the women unto the custody of Hegai the king's chamberlain, keeper of the
women, and let their ointments be given them 4 and let the maiden that pleaseth the king be queen
instead of Vashti.' And the thing pleased the king and he did so. [S]

**5 There was a certain Jew in Shushan fortress whose name was Mordecai, the son of Jair,
the son of Shimei, the son of Kish, a Benjamite**

כִּי־כֵן דְּבַר הַמֶּלֶךְ לִפְנֵי כָּל־יֹדְעֵי דָּת וָדִין.

יד וְהַקָּרֹב אֵלָיו כַּרְשְׁנָא שֵׁתָר אַדְמָתָא תַרְשִׁישׁ מֶרֶס מַרְסְנָא מְמוּכָן שִׁבְעַת שָׂרֵי פָּרַס וּמָדַי רֹאֵי פְּנֵי הַמֶּלֶךְ הַיֹּשְׁבִים רִאשֹׁנָה בַּמַּלְכוּת.

טו כְּדָת מַה־לַּעֲשׂוֹת בַּמַּלְכָּה וַשְׁתִּי עַל אֲשֶׁר לֹא־עָשְׂתָה אֶת־מַאֲמַר הַמֶּלֶךְ אֲחַשְׁוֵרוֹשׁ בְּיַד הַסָּרִיסִים. [ס]

טז וַיֹּאמֶר מוֹמֻכָן (מְמוּכָן) לִפְנֵי הַמֶּלֶךְ וְהַשָּׂרִים לֹא עַל־הַמֶּלֶךְ לְבַדּוֹ עָוְתָה וַשְׁתִּי הַמַּלְכָּה: כִּי עַל־כָּל־הַשָּׂרִים וְעַל־כָּל־הָעַמִּים אֲשֶׁר בְּכָל־מְדִינוֹת הַמֶּלֶךְ אֲחַשְׁוֵרוֹשׁ. יז כִּי־יֵצֵא דְבַר־הַמַּלְכָּה עַל־כָּל־הַנָּשִׁים לְהַבְזוֹת בַּעְלֵיהֶן בְּעֵינֵיהֶן: בְּאָמְרָם הַמֶּלֶךְ אֲחַשְׁוֵרוֹשׁ אָמַר לְהָבִיא אֶת־וַשְׁתִּי הַמַּלְכָּה לְפָנָיו וְלֹא־בָאָה. יח וְהַיּוֹם הַזֶּה תֹּאמַרְנָה שָׂרוֹת פָּרַס־וּמָדַי אֲשֶׁר שָׁמְעוּ אֶת־דְּבַר הַמַּלְכָּה לְכֹל שָׂרֵי הַמֶּלֶךְ וּכְדַי בִּזָּיוֹן וָקָצֶף. יט אִם־עַל־הַמֶּלֶךְ טוֹב יֵצֵא דְבַר־מַלְכוּת מִלְּפָנָיו וְיִכָּתֵב בְּדָתֵי פָרַס־וּמָדַי וְלֹא יַעֲבוֹר אֲשֶׁר לֹא־תָבוֹא וַשְׁתִּי לִפְנֵי הַמֶּלֶךְ אֲחַשְׁוֵרוֹשׁ וּמַלְכוּתָהּ יִתֵּן הַמֶּלֶךְ לִרְעוּתָהּ הַטּוֹבָה מִמֶּנָּה. כ וְנִשְׁמַע פִּתְגָם הַמֶּלֶךְ אֲשֶׁר־יַעֲשֶׂה בְּכָל־מַלְכוּתוֹ כִּי רַבָּה הִיא וְכָל־הַנָּשִׁים יִתְּנוּ יְקָר לְבַעְלֵיהֶן לְמִגָּדוֹל וְעַד־קָטָן. כא וַיִּיטַב הַדָּבָר בְּעֵינֵי הַמֶּלֶךְ וְהַשָּׂרִים; וַיַּעַשׂ הַמֶּלֶךְ כִּדְבַר מְמוּכָן. כב וַיִּשְׁלַח סְפָרִים אֶל־כָּל־מְדִינוֹת הַמֶּלֶךְ אֶל־מְדִינָה וּמְדִינָה כִּכְתָבָהּ וְאֶל־עַם וָעָם כִּלְשׁוֹנוֹ לִהְיוֹת כָּל־אִישׁ שֹׂרֵר בְּבֵיתוֹ וּמְדַבֵּר כִּלְשׁוֹן עַמּוֹ. [ס]

פֶּרֶק ב

א אַחַר הַדְּבָרִים הָאֵלֶּה כְּשֹׁךְ חֲמַת הַמֶּלֶךְ אֲחַשְׁוֵרוֹשׁ זָכַר אֶת־וַשְׁתִּי וְאֵת אֲשֶׁר־עָשָׂתָה וְאֵת אֲשֶׁר־נִגְזַר עָלֶיהָ. ב וַיֹּאמְרוּ נַעֲרֵי־הַמֶּלֶךְ מְשָׁרְתָיו יְבַקְשׁוּ לַמֶּלֶךְ נְעָרוֹת בְּתוּלוֹת טוֹבוֹת מַרְאֶה. ג וְיַפְקֵד הַמֶּלֶךְ פְּקִידִים בְּכָל־מְדִינוֹת מַלְכוּתוֹ וְיִקְבְּצוּ אֶת־כָּל־נַעֲרָה־בְתוּלָה טוֹבַת מַרְאֶה אֶל־שׁוּשַׁן הַבִּירָה אֶל־בֵּית הַנָּשִׁים אֶל־יַד הֵגֶא סְרִיס הַמֶּלֶךְ שֹׁמֵר הַנָּשִׁים וְנָתוֹן תַּמְרוּקֵיהֶן. ד וְהַנַּעֲרָה אֲשֶׁר תִּיטַב בְּעֵינֵי הַמֶּלֶךְ תִּמְלֹךְ תַּחַת וַשְׁתִּי; וַיִּיטַב הַדָּבָר בְּעֵינֵי הַמֶּלֶךְ וַיַּעַשׂ כֵּן. [ס]

ה אִישׁ יְהוּדִי הָיָה בְּשׁוּשַׁן הַבִּירָה וּשְׁמוֹ מָרְדֳּכַי בֶּן יָאִיר בֶּן־שִׁמְעִי בֶּן־קִישׁ אִישׁ יְמִינִי.

6 who had been carried away from Jerusalem with the captives that were carried away with Jeconiah king of Judah whom Nebuchadnezzar the king of Babylon had carried away. 7 And he brought up

Hadassah	Esther
(his uncle's daughter,)	for she had neither father nor mother

and the maiden was of beautiful form and fair to look on

and when her father and mother were dead
Mordecai adopted her as his own daughter.

8 And so it was when the king's word and his decree were published and when many maidens were gathered together unto Shushan fortress (to the custody of Hegai) that Esther was taken

into the king's house	(to the custody of Hegai, keeper of the women)
9 and the maiden pleased him [*i.e. Ahasuerus*]	[*i.e. Hegai*]

and she obtained kindness of him.

and he speedily gave her her ointments with her portions and the seven maidens who were due to be given her out of the king's house, and he advanced her and her maidens to the best place in the house of the women.

(10 Esther did not reveal her people or her kindred, for Mordecai had charged her that she should not tell it.)

(11 And Mordecai walked every day before the court of the women's house to know how Esther did and what would become of her.)

12 Now when the turn of every maiden came to go in to King Ahasuerus, after that it had been done to her according to the law for the women twelve months (for thus were the days of their anointing carried out: six months with myrrh oil and six months with sweet odours and other feminine ointments), 13 then when a maiden came unto the king, whatsoever she desired was given her to go with her out of the house of the women unto the king's house. 14 In the evening she would go and next morning would return to the second house of the women, to the custody of Shaashgaz, the king's chamberlain who kept the concubines, and she would not return to the king unless the

ו אֲשֶׁר הָגְלָה מִירוּשָׁלַיִם עִם־הַגֹּלָה אֲשֶׁר הָגְלְתָה עִם יְכָנְיָה מֶלֶךְ־יְהוּדָה אֲשֶׁר
הֶגְלָה נְבוּכַדְנֶצַּר מֶלֶךְ בָּבֶל. ז וַיְהִי אֹמֵן

| הִיא אֶסְתֵּר | אֶת־הֲדַסָּה |
| כִּי אֵין לָהּ אָב וָאֵם | בַּת־דֹּדוֹ |

וְהַנַּעֲרָה יְפַת־תֹּאַר וְטוֹבַת מַרְאֶה

| | וּבְמוֹת אָבִיהָ וְאִמָּהּ לְקָחָהּ מָרְדֳּכַי לוֹ לְבַת.

ח וַיְהִי בְּהִשָּׁמַע דְּבַר־הַמֶּלֶךְ וְדָתוֹ וּבְהִקָּבֵץ נְעָרוֹת רַבּוֹת אֶל־שׁוּשַׁן הַבִּירָה
אֶל־יַד הֵגַי וַתִּלָּקַח אֶסְתֵּר

| אֶל־יַד הֵגַי שֹׁמֵר הַנָּשִׁים. | אֶל־בֵּית הַמֶּלֶךְ |

| | ט וַתִּיטַב הַנַּעֲרָה בְעֵינָיו

| וַתִּשָּׂא חֶסֶד לְפָנָיו

וַיְבַהֵל אֶת־תַּמְרוּקֶיהָ וְאֶת־מָנוֹתֶהָ לָתֵת
לָהּ וְאֵת שֶׁבַע הַנְּעָרוֹת הָרְאֻיוֹת לָתֶת־לָהּ
מִבֵּית הַמֶּלֶךְ וַיְשַׁנֶּהָ וְאֶת־נַעֲרוֹתֶיהָ לְטוֹב
בֵּית הַנָּשִׁים.

י לֹא־הִגִּידָה אֶסְתֵּר
אֶת־עַמָּהּ וְאֶת־מוֹלַדְתָּהּ
כִּי מָרְדֳּכַי צִוָּה עָלֶיהָ
אֲשֶׁר לֹא־תַגִּיד.

יא וּבְכָל־יוֹם וָיוֹם מָרְדֳּכַי מִתְהַלֵּךְ לִפְנֵי חֲצַר בֵּית־
הַנָּשִׁים לָדַעַת אֶת־שְׁלוֹם אֶסְתֵּר וּמַה־יֵּעָשֶׂה בָּהּ.

יב וּבְהַגִּיעַ תֹּר נַעֲרָה וְנַעֲרָה לָבוֹא אֶל־הַמֶּלֶךְ
אֲחַשְׁוֵרוֹשׁ מִקֵּץ הֱיוֹת לָהּ כְּדָת הַנָּשִׁים שְׁנֵים
עָשָׂר חֹדֶשׁ כִּי כֵּן יִמְלְאוּ יְמֵי מְרוּקֵיהֶן שִׁשָּׁה
חֳדָשִׁים בְּשֶׁמֶן הַמֹּר וְשִׁשָּׁה חֳדָשִׁים בַּבְּשָׂמִים
וּבְתַמְרוּקֵי הַנָּשִׁים. יג וּבָזֶה הַנַּעֲרָה בָּאָה אֶל־
הַמֶּלֶךְ אֵת כָּל־אֲשֶׁר תֹּאמַר יִנָּתֵן לָהּ לָבוֹא עִמָּהּ
מִבֵּית הַנָּשִׁים עַד־בֵּית הַמֶּלֶךְ. יד בָּעֶרֶב הִיא
בָאָה וּבַבֹּקֶר הִיא שָׁבָה אֶל־בֵּית הַנָּשִׁים שֵׁנִי
אֶל־יַד שַׁעַשְׁגַז סְרִיס הַמֶּלֶךְ שֹׁמֵר הַפִּילַגְשִׁים
לֹא־תָבוֹא עוֹד אֶל־הַמֶּלֶךְ כִּי אִם־חָפֵץ בָּהּ

king delighted in her and she was called for by name.) 15 Now when came the turn of Esther

(the daughter of Abihail,

> (the uncle of Mordecai who took her as his daughter)

to go to the king, she only needed what Hegai the king's chamberlain, keeper of the women, decided.

(Everyone who saw Esther adored her.)

16 So Esther was taken unto King Ahasuerus into his house royal in the tenth month

(which is the month of Tevet) | (in the seventh year of his reign).

17 And the king loved Esther above all the women and she obtained grace and favour in his sight more than all the virgins so that he set the royal crown upon her head and made her queen instead of Vashti. 18 Then the king made a great feast unto all his princes and his servants, even Esther's feast, and he made a release to the provinces and gave gifts according to the bounty of the king.

19 (And the virgins were gathered again . . .)

(And Mordecai sat in the king's gate . . .)

20 Esther had not yet made known her kindred nor her people as Mordecai had charged her, for Esther did the commandment of Mordecai just as when she was brought up with him. [S]

21 In those days, while Mordecai sat in the king's gate, Bigthan and Teresh, two of the king's chamberlains that guarded the door, were wroth and sought to lay hands on the king Ahasuerus. 22 And the thing became known to Mordecai who told it unto Queen Esther, and Esther told the king thereof in Mordecai's name. 23 And when inquisition was made of the matter and it was found to be so, they were both hanged on a tree and it was written in the *Book of Chronicles* before the king. [S]

Chapter 3

1 After these events King Ahasuerus promoted Haman the son of Hammedatha the Agagite and advanced him and set his seat above all the princes that were with him. 2 And all the king's servants that were in the king's gate bowed down and prostrated themselves before Haman for the king had so commanded concerning him. But Mordecai neither bowed down nor prostrated himself before him. 3 Then the king's servants that were in the king's gate said unto Mordecai: 'Why do you transgress the king's commandment?' 4 Now it came to pass that they spoke daily unto him and he hearkened not unto them, so they told Haman to see whether Mordecai's words would be allowed to stand, for he

הַמֶּלֶךְ וְנִקְרְאָה בְשֵׁם. טו וּבְהַגִּיעַ תֹּר־אֶסְתֵּר בַּת־אֲבִיחַיִל

דֹּד מָרְדֳּכַי אֲשֶׁר לָקַח־לוֹ לְבַת

לָבוֹא אֶל־הַמֶּלֶךְ לֹא בִקְשָׁה דָּבָר כִּי אִם אֶת־אֲשֶׁר יֹאמַר הֵגַי סְרִיס־הַמֶּלֶךְ שֹׁמֵר הַנָּשִׁים

וַתְּהִי אֶסְתֵּר נֹשֵׂאת חֵן בְּעֵינֵי כָּל־רֹאֶיהָ.

טז וַתִּלָּקַח אֶסְתֵּר אֶל־הַמֶּלֶךְ אֲחַשְׁוֵרוֹשׁ אֶל־בֵּית מַלְכוּתוֹ בַּחֹדֶשׁ הָעֲשִׂירִי

הוּא־חֹדֶשׁ טֵבֵת | בִּשְׁנַת־שֶׁבַע לְמַלְכוּתוֹ.

יז וַיֶּאֱהַב הַמֶּלֶךְ אֶת־אֶסְתֵּר מִכָּל־הַנָּשִׁים וַתִּשָּׂא־חֵן וָחֶסֶד לְפָנָיו מִכָּל־הַבְּתוּלוֹת וַיָּשֶׂם כֶּתֶר־מַלְכוּת בְּרֹאשָׁהּ וַיַּמְלִיכֶהָ תַּחַת וַשְׁתִּי. יח וַיַּעַשׂ הַמֶּלֶךְ מִשְׁתֶּה גָדוֹל לְכָל־שָׂרָיו וַעֲבָדָיו אֵת מִשְׁתֵּה אֶסְתֵּר וַהֲנָחָה לַמְּדִינוֹת עָשָׂה וַיִּתֵּן מַשְׂאֵת כְּיַד הַמֶּלֶךְ.

יט וּבְהִקָּבֵץ בְּתוּלוֹת שֵׁנִית |

וּמָרְדֳּכַי יֹשֵׁב בְּשַׁעַר־הַמֶּלֶךְ.

כ אֵין אֶסְתֵּר מַגֶּדֶת מוֹלַדְתָּהּ וְאֶת־עַמָּהּ כַּאֲשֶׁר צִוָּה עָלֶיהָ מָרְדֳּכַי וְאֶת־מַאֲמַר מָרְדֳּכַי אֶסְתֵּר עֹשָׂה כַּאֲשֶׁר הָיְתָה בְאָמְנָה אִתּוֹ. [ס]

כא בַּיָּמִים הָהֵם וּמָרְדֳּכַי יוֹשֵׁב בְּשַׁעַר־הַמֶּלֶךְ קָצַף בִּגְתָן וָתֶרֶשׁ שְׁנֵי־סָרִיסֵי הַמֶּלֶךְ מִשֹּׁמְרֵי הַסַּף וַיְבַקְשׁוּ לִשְׁלֹחַ יָד בַּמֶּלֶךְ אֲחַשְׁוֵרֹשׁ. כב וַיִּוָּדַע הַדָּבָר לְמָרְדֳּכַי וַיַּגֵּד לְאֶסְתֵּר הַמַּלְכָּה וַתֹּאמֶר אֶסְתֵּר לַמֶּלֶךְ בְּשֵׁם מָרְדֳּכָי. כג וַיְבֻקַּשׁ הַדָּבָר וַיִּמָּצֵא וַיִּתָּלוּ שְׁנֵיהֶם עַל־עֵץ וַיִּכָּתֵב בְּסֵפֶר דִּבְרֵי הַיָּמִים לִפְנֵי הַמֶּלֶךְ. [ס]

פֶּרֶק ג

א אַחַר הַדְּבָרִים הָאֵלֶּה גִּדַּל הַמֶּלֶךְ אֲחַשְׁוֵרוֹשׁ אֶת־הָמָן בֶּן־הַמְּדָתָא הָאֲגָגִי וַיְנַשְּׂאֵהוּ וַיָּשֶׂם אֶת־כִּסְאוֹ מֵעַל כָּל־הַשָּׂרִים אֲשֶׁר אִתּוֹ. ב וְכָל־עַבְדֵי הַמֶּלֶךְ אֲשֶׁר־בְּשַׁעַר הַמֶּלֶךְ כֹּרְעִים וּמִשְׁתַּחֲוִים לְהָמָן כִּי־כֵן צִוָּה־לוֹ הַמֶּלֶךְ וּמָרְדֳּכַי לֹא יִכְרַע וְלֹא יִשְׁתַּחֲוֶה. ג וַיֹּאמְרוּ עַבְדֵי הַמֶּלֶךְ אֲשֶׁר־בְּשַׁעַר הַמֶּלֶךְ לְמָרְדֳּכַי מַדּוּעַ אַתָּה עוֹבֵר אֵת מִצְוַת הַמֶּלֶךְ. ד וַיְהִי באמרם (כְּאָמְרָם) אֵלָיו יוֹם וָיוֹם וְלֹא שָׁמַע אֲלֵיהֶם וַיַּגִּידוּ לְהָמָן לִרְאוֹת הֲיַעַמְדוּ דִּבְרֵי מָרְדֳּכַי כִּי־הִגִּיד

had told them he was a Jew. 5 And when Haman saw that Mordecai neither bowed down nor prostrated himself before him then was Haman full of wrath. 6 But it seemed contemptible in his eyes to lay hands on Mordecai alone, for they had made known to him the people of Mordecai, so Haman sought to destroy all the Jews throughout the whole kingdom of Ahasuerus—the people of Mordecai.

> 7 In the first month (i.e. the month of Niysan) (in
> the twelfth year of King Ahasuerus) they cast *pur*
> (i.e. the *lot*) before Haman [to determine] the day
> and the month [until it fell on] the twelfth month
> (which is the month of Adar). [S]

8 And Haman said unto King Ahasuerus: 'There is a certain people scattered abroad and dispersed among the peoples in all the provinces of thy kingdom and their laws are diverse from those of every people, neither keep they the king's laws, therefore it profiteth not the king to suffer them. 9 If it please the king let it be written that they be destroyed and I will pay ten thousand talents of silver into the hands of those that have the charge of the king's business to bring it into the king's treasuries.' 10 And the king took his ring from his hand and gave it unto Haman the son of Hammedatha the Agagite, the Jews' enemy. 11 And the king said unto Haman: 'The silver and the people are thine to do with as it seemeth good to thee.' 12 Then were the king's scribes called in the first month on the thirteenth day thereof and there was written according to all that Haman commanded

to the king's satraps and to the governors that were over every province and to the princes of every people;

to every province according to the writing thereof, and to every people after their language;

in the name of king Ahasuerus was it written and it was sealed with the king's ring.

13 And documents were sent by posts into all the king's provinces to destroy, to slay and to cause to perish all Jews, young and old, little children and women, in one day even, upon the thirteenth day of the twelfth month which is the month Adar and to take the spoil of them for a prey.

14 The copy of the text for release as a decree in every province was to be published for all peoples so they should be ready against that day.

15 The posts went forth in haste by the king's commandment and the decree was given out in Shushan castle.

And the king and Haman sat down to drink but the city of Shushan was perplexed. [S]

Chapter 4

1 Now when Mordecai knew all that was done Mordecai rent his clothes and put on sackcloth and ashes and went out into the midst of the city and cried with a loud and a bitter cry. 2 And he came even as far as the king's gate (for none might enter within the king's gate clothed in sackcloth).

3 In every province wherever the king's law and his decree came there was great mourning among the Jews and fasting and weeping and wailing, and many lay in sackcloth and ashes.

4 And Esther's maidens and her chamberlains came and told this to her and the queen was much pained and sent raiment to clothe Mordecai and to take his sackcloth from him but he accepted it not.

5 And Esther called for Hathach, one of the king's chamberlains whom he had appointed to attend upon her, and charged him to go to Mordecai to know what this was and why it was.

לָהֶם אֲשֶׁר־הוּא יְהוּדִי. ה וַיַּרְא הָמָן כִּי־אֵין מָרְדֳּכַי כֹּרֵעַ וּמִשְׁתַּחֲוֶה לוֹ וַיִּמָּלֵא הָמָן חֵמָה.

ו וַיִּבֶז בְּעֵינָיו לִשְׁלֹחַ יָד בְּמָרְדֳּכַי לְבַדּוֹ כִּי־הִגִּידוּ לוֹ אֶת־עַם מָרְדֳּכָי וַיְבַקֵּשׁ הָמָן לְהַשְׁמִיד אֶת־כָּל־הַיְּהוּדִים אֲשֶׁר בְּכָל־מַלְכוּת אֲחַשְׁוֵרוֹשׁ עַם מָרְדֳּכָי.

ז בַּחֹדֶשׁ הָרִאשׁוֹן הוּא־חֹדֶשׁ נִיסָן בִּשְׁנַת
שְׁתֵּים עֶשְׂרֵה לַמֶּלֶךְ אֲחַשְׁוֵרוֹשׁ הִפִּיל פּוּר הוּא
הַגּוֹרָל לִפְנֵי הָמָן מִיּוֹם לְיוֹם וּמֵחֹדֶשׁ לְחֹדֶשׁ
שְׁנֵים־עָשָׂר הוּא־חֹדֶשׁ אֲדָר.   [ס]

ח וַיֹּאמֶר הָמָן לַמֶּלֶךְ אֲחַשְׁוֵרוֹשׁ יֶשְׁנוֹ עַם־אֶחָד מְפֻזָּר וּמְפֹרָד בֵּין הָעַמִּים בְּכֹל מְדִינוֹת מַלְכוּתֶךָ וְדָתֵיהֶם שֹׁנוֹת מִכָּל־עָם וְאֶת־דָּתֵי הַמֶּלֶךְ אֵינָם עֹשִׂים וְלַמֶּלֶךְ אֵין־שֹׁוֶה לְהַנִּיחָם. ט אִם־עַל־הַמֶּלֶךְ טוֹב יִכָּתֵב לְאַבְּדָם וַעֲשֶׂרֶת אֲלָפִים כִּכַּר־כֶּסֶף אֶשְׁקוֹל עַל־יְדֵי עֹשֵׂי הַמְּלָאכָה לְהָבִיא אֶל־גִּנְזֵי הַמֶּלֶךְ. י וַיָּסַר הַמֶּלֶךְ אֶת־טַבַּעְתּוֹ מֵעַל יָדוֹ וַיִּתְּנָהּ לְהָמָן בֶּן־הַמְּדָתָא הָאֲגָגִי צֹרֵר הַיְּהוּדִים.

יא וַיֹּאמֶר הַמֶּלֶךְ לְהָמָן הַכֶּסֶף נָתוּן לָךְ וְהָעָם לַעֲשׂוֹת בּוֹ כַּטּוֹב בְּעֵינֶיךָ. יב וַיִּקָּרְאוּ סֹפְרֵי הַמֶּלֶךְ בַּחֹדֶשׁ הָרִאשׁוֹן בִּשְׁלוֹשָׁה עָשָׂר יוֹם בּוֹ וַיִּכָּתֵב כְּכָל־אֲשֶׁר־צִוָּה הָמָן

| מְדִינָה וּמְדִינָה כִּכְתָבָהּ וְעַם וָעָם כִּלְשׁוֹנוֹ: | אֶל אֲחַשְׁדַּרְפְּנֵי־הַמֶּלֶךְ וְאֶל־הַפַּחוֹת אֲשֶׁר עַל־מְדִינָה וּמְדִינָה וְאֶל־שָׂרֵי עַם וָעָם |

בְּשֵׁם הַמֶּלֶךְ אֲחַשְׁוֵרֹשׁ נִכְתָּב וְנֶחְתָּם בְּטַבַּעַת הַמֶּלֶךְ

| טו הָרָצִים יָצְאוּ דְחוּפִים בִּדְבַר הַמֶּלֶךְ וְהַדָּת נִתְּנָה בְּשׁוּשַׁן הַבִּירָה | יד פַּתְשֶׁגֶן הַכְּתָב לְהִנָּתֵן דָּת בְּכָל־מְדִי־נָה וּמְדִינָה גָּלוּי לְכָל־הָעַמִּים לִהְיוֹת עֲתִדִים לַיּוֹם הַזֶּה. | יג וְנִשְׁלוֹחַ סְפָרִים בְּיַד הָרָצִים אֶל־כָּל־מְדִינוֹת הַמֶּלֶךְ לְהַשְׁמִיד לַהֲרֹג וּלְאַבֵּד אֶת־כָּל־הַיְּהוּדִים מִנַּעַר וְעַד־זָקֵן טַף וְנָשִׁים בְּיוֹם אֶחָד בִּשְׁלוֹשָׁה עָשָׂר לְחֹדֶשׁ שְׁנֵים־עָשָׂר הוּא־חֹדֶשׁ אֲדָר וּשְׁלָלָם לָבוֹז. |

וְהַמֶּלֶךְ וְהָמָן יָשְׁבוּ לִשְׁתּוֹת וְהָעִיר שׁוּשָׁן נָבוֹכָה.   [ס]

פרק ד

| ג וּבְכָל־מְדִינָה וּמְדִינָה מְקוֹם אֲשֶׁר דְּבַר־הַמֶּלֶךְ וְדָתוֹ מַגִּיעַ אֵבֶל גָּדוֹל לַיְּהוּדִים וְצוֹם וּבְכִי וּמִסְפֵּד שַׂק וָאֵפֶר יֻצַּע לָרַבִּים. | א וּמָרְדֳּכַי יָדַע אֶת־כָּל־אֲשֶׁר נַעֲשָׂה וַיִּקְרַע מָרְדֳּכַי אֶת־בְּגָדָיו וַיִּלְבַּשׁ שַׂק וָאֵפֶר וַיֵּצֵא בְּתוֹךְ הָעִיר וַיִּזְעַק זְעָקָה גְדוֹלָה וּמָרָה. ב וַיָּבוֹא עַד לִפְנֵי שַׁעַר־הַמֶּלֶךְ כִּי אֵין לָבוֹא אֶל־שַׁעַר הַמֶּלֶךְ בִּלְבוּשׁ שָׂק. |

| ה וַתִּקְרָא אֶסְתֵּר לַהֲתָךְ מִסָּרִיסֵי הַמֶּלֶךְ אֲשֶׁר הֶעֱמִיד לְפָנֶיהָ וַתְּצַוֵּהוּ עַל־מָרְדֳּכָי לָדַעַת מַה־זֶּה וְעַל־מַה־זֶּה. | ד וַתָּבוֹאינָה (וַתָּבוֹאנָה) נַעֲרוֹת אֶסְתֵּר וְסָרִיסֶיהָ וַיַּגִּידוּ לָהּ וַתִּתְחַלְחַל הַמַּלְכָּה מְאֹד וַתִּשְׁלַח בְּגָדִים לְהַלְבִּישׁ אֶת־מָרְדֳּכַי וּלְהָסִיר שַׂקּוֹ מֵעָלָיו וְלֹא קִבֵּל. |

6 So Hathach went forth to Mordecai unto the main street of the city which was before the king's gate. 7 And Mordecai told him all that had happened unto him and the exact sum of the money that Haman had promised to pay into the king's treasuries for the Jews to destroy them. 8 Also he gave him the copy of the writing of the decree that was given out in Shushan to destroy them to show it unto Esther and to declare it unto her and charge her that she should go in unto the king to make supplication unto him and to entreat before him for her people. 9 And Hathach came and told Esther the words of Mordecai. 10 Then Esther spoke unto Hathach and gave him a message for Mordecai: 11 'All the king's servants and the people of the king's provinces do know that every man or woman who shall come unto the king into the inner court who is not called, there is one law for him: that he be put to death, except to whom the king shall hold out the golden sceptre that he may live, and I have not been called to come in unto the king these thirty days.' 12 And they told Mordecai Esther's words. 13 Then Mordecai bade them to reply unto Esther: 'Think not with thyself that thou shalt escape in the king's house more than all the Jews. 14 For if thou altogether holdest thy peace at this time then will relief and deliverance arise to the Jews from another place but thou and thy father's house will perish; and who knoweth whether thou art not come to royal estate for such a time as this?' 15 Then Esther bade them return answer unto Mordecai: 16 'Go gather together all the Jews that are present in Shushan and fast ye for me and neither eat nor drink three days night or day; I also and my maidens will fast in like manner; and so will I go in unto the king which is not according to the law; and if I perish I perish.' 17 So Mordecai went his way and did according to all that Esther had commanded him.

Chapter 5

1 Now it came to pass on the third day that Esther put on her royal apparel and stood in the inner court of the king's house in sight of the king's house and the king sat upon his royal throne in the royal house in sight of the entrance of the house. 2 And it was so when the king saw Esther the queen standing in the court that she obtained favour in his sight and the king held out to Esther the golden sceptre that was in his hand. So Esther drew near and touched the top of the sceptre. 3 Then said the king unto her: 'What wilt thou, Queen Esther? for whatever thy request even to the half of the kingdom it shall be given thee.'

4 And Esther said: 'If it please the king let the king and Haman come this day unto the party that I have prepared for him.' 5 Then the king said: 'Cause Haman to hurry so it may be done as Esther hath said.' So the king and Haman came to the party that Esther had prepared. 6 And the king said to Esther at the party of wine: 'Whatever thy petition it shall be granted thee and whatever thy request even to the half of the kingdom it shall be performed.'

7 Then answered Esther and said: 'My petition and my request is that 8 if I have found favour in the sight of the king and if it please the king to grant my petition and to perform my request let the king and Haman come to the party that I shall prepare for them and I will do tomorrow as the king hath said.' 9 Then went Haman forth that day full of joy and glad of heart but when Haman saw that Mordecai in the king's gate neither stood up nor moved for him, Haman was filled with wrath against Mordecai. 10 Haman nevertheless refrained himself and went home and sent and fetched his friends and Zeresh his wife. 11 And Haman recounted unto them the glory of his riches and the multitude of his children and everything as to how the king had promoted him and how he had advanced him above the princes and servants of the king. 12 Haman said moreover: 'Yea Esther the queen did let no man come in with the king unto the party that she had prepared but myself; and tomorrow also am I invited by her together with the king. 13 Yet all this availeth me nothing so long as I see Mordecai the Jew sitting at the king's gate.' 14 Then said Zeresh his wife and all his friends unto him: 'Let a gallows be made of fifty cubits high and in the morning speak thou unto the king that Mordecai may be hanged thereon; then go thou in merrily with the king unto the banquet.' And the thing pleased Haman and he caused the gallows to be made. [S]

ו וַיֵּצֵא הֲתָךְ אֶל־מָרְדֳּכָי אֶל־רְחוֹב הָעִיר אֲשֶׁר לִפְנֵי שַׁעַר־הַמֶּלֶךְ. ז וַיַּגֶּד־לוֹ מָרְדֳּכַי אֵת כָּל־אֲשֶׁר
קָרָהוּ וְאֵת פָּרָשַׁת הַכֶּסֶף אֲשֶׁר אָמַר הָמָן לִשְׁקוֹל עַל־גִּנְזֵי הַמֶּלֶךְ בַּיְּהוּדִים (בַּיְּהוּדִים) לְאַבְּדָם.
ח וְאֶת־פַּתְשֶׁגֶן כְּתָב־הַדָּת אֲשֶׁר־נִתַּן בְּשׁוּשָׁן לְהַשְׁמִידָם נָתַן לוֹ לְהַרְאוֹת אֶת־אֶסְתֵּר וּלְהַגִּיד לָהּ
וּלְצַוּוֹת עָלֶיהָ לָבוֹא אֶל־הַמֶּלֶךְ לְהִתְחַנֶּן־לוֹ וּלְבַקֵּשׁ מִלְּפָנָיו עַל־עַמָּהּ. ט וַיָּבוֹא הֲתָךְ וַיַּגֵּד לְאֶסְתֵּר אֵת
דִּבְרֵי מָרְדֳּכָי. י וַתֹּאמֶר אֶסְתֵּר לַהֲתָךְ וַתְּצַוֵּהוּ אֶל־מָרְדֳּכָי. יא כָּל־עַבְדֵי הַמֶּלֶךְ וְעַם־מְדִינוֹת הַמֶּלֶךְ
יֹדְעִים אֲשֶׁר כָּל־אִישׁ וְאִשָּׁה אֲשֶׁר יָבוֹא־אֶל־הַמֶּלֶךְ אֶל־הֶחָצֵר הַפְּנִימִית אֲשֶׁר לֹא־יִקָּרֵא אַחַת דָּתוֹ
לְהָמִית לְבַד מֵאֲשֶׁר יוֹשִׁיט־לוֹ הַמֶּלֶךְ אֶת־שַׁרְבִיט הַזָּהָב וְחָיָה וַאֲנִי לֹא נִקְרֵאתִי לָבוֹא אֶל־הַמֶּלֶךְ זֶה
שְׁלוֹשִׁים יוֹם. יב וַיַּגִּידוּ לְמָרְדֳּכָי אֵת דִּבְרֵי אֶסְתֵּר. יג וַיֹּאמֶר מָרְדֳּכַי לְהָשִׁיב אֶל־אֶסְתֵּר אַל־תְּדַמִּי
בְנַפְשֵׁךְ לְהִמָּלֵט בֵּית־הַמֶּלֶךְ מִכָּל־הַיְּהוּדִים. יד כִּי אִם־הַחֲרֵשׁ תַּחֲרִישִׁי בָּעֵת הַזֹּאת רֶוַח וְהַצָּלָה
יַעֲמוֹד לַיְּהוּדִים מִמָּקוֹם אַחֵר וְאַתְּ וּבֵית־אָבִיךְ תֹּאבֵדוּ וּמִי יוֹדֵעַ אִם־לְעֵת כָּזֹאת הִגַּעַתְּ לַמַּלְכוּת.
טו וַתֹּאמֶר אֶסְתֵּר לְהָשִׁיב אֶל־מָרְדֳּכָי. טז לֵךְ כְּנוֹס אֶת־כָּל־הַיְּהוּדִים הַנִּמְצְאִים בְּשׁוּשָׁן וְצוּמוּ עָלַי
וְאַל־תֹּאכְלוּ וְאַל־תִּשְׁתּוּ שְׁלֹשֶׁת יָמִים לַיְלָה וָיוֹם גַּם־אֲנִי וְנַעֲרֹתַי אָצוּם כֵּן וּבְכֵן אָבוֹא אֶל־הַמֶּלֶךְ
אֲשֶׁר לֹא־כַדָּת וְכַאֲשֶׁר אָבַדְתִּי אָבָדְתִּי. יז וַיַּעֲבֹר מָרְדֳּכָי וַיַּעַשׂ כְּכֹל אֲשֶׁר־צִוְּתָה עָלָיו אֶסְתֵּר.

פֶּרֶק ה

א וַיְהִי בַּיּוֹם הַשְּׁלִישִׁי וַתִּלְבַּשׁ אֶסְתֵּר מַלְכוּת וַתַּעֲמֹד בַּחֲצַר בֵּית־הַמֶּלֶךְ הַפְּנִימִית נֹכַח בֵּית הַמֶּלֶךְ וְהַמֶּ־
לֶךְ יוֹשֵׁב עַל־כִּסֵּא מַלְכוּתוֹ בְּבֵית הַמַּלְכוּת נֹכַח פֶּתַח הַבָּיִת. ב וַיְהִי כִרְאוֹת הַמֶּלֶךְ אֶת־אֶסְתֵּר הַמַּלְכָּה
עֹמֶדֶת בֶּחָצֵר נָשְׂאָה חֵן בְּעֵינָיו וַיּוֹשֶׁט הַמֶּלֶךְ לְאֶסְתֵּר אֶת־שַׁרְבִיט הַזָּהָב אֲשֶׁר בְּיָדוֹ וַתִּקְרַב אֶסְתֵּר וַתִּגַּע
בְּרֹאשׁ הַשַּׁרְבִיט. ג וַיֹּאמֶר לָהּ הַמֶּלֶךְ מַה־לָּךְ אֶסְתֵּר הַמַּלְכָּה וּמַה־בַּקָּשָׁתֵךְ עַד־חֲצִי הַמַּלְכוּת וְיִנָּתֵן לָךְ.

ד וַתֹּאמֶר אֶסְתֵּר אִם־
עַל־הַמֶּלֶךְ טוֹב יָבוֹא
הַמֶּלֶךְ וְהָמָן הַיּוֹם אֶל־
הַמִּשְׁתֶּה אֲשֶׁר־עָשִׂיתִי
לוֹ. ה וַיֹּאמֶר הַמֶּלֶךְ
מַהֲרוּ אֶת־הָמָן לַעֲשׂוֹת
אֶת־דְּבַר אֶסְתֵּר וַיָּבֹא
הַמֶּלֶךְ וְהָמָן אֶל־הַמִּ־
שְׁתֶּה אֲשֶׁר־עָשְׂתָה
אֶסְתֵּר. ו וַיֹּאמֶר הַמֶּלֶךְ
לְאֶסְתֵּר בְּמִשְׁתֵּה הַיַּיִן
מַה־שְּׁאֵלָתֵךְ וְיִנָּתֵן לָךְ
וּמַה־בַּקָּשָׁתֵךְ עַד־חֲצִי
הַמַּלְכוּת וְתֵעָשׂ.

ז וַתַּעַן אֶסְתֵּר וַתֹּאמַר שְׁאֵלָתִי וּבַקָּשָׁתִי. ח אִם־מָצָאתִי חֵן בְּעֵינֵי הַמֶּלֶךְ
וְאִם־עַל־הַמֶּלֶךְ טוֹב לָתֵת אֶת־שְׁאֵלָתִי וְלַעֲשׂוֹת אֶת־בַּקָּשָׁתִי יָבוֹא הַמֶּלֶךְ
וְהָמָן אֶל־הַמִּשְׁתֶּה אֲשֶׁר אֶעֱשֶׂה לָהֶם וּמָחָר אֶעֱשֶׂה כִּדְבַר הַמֶּלֶךְ.
ט וַיֵּצֵא הָמָן בַּיּוֹם הַהוּא שָׂמֵחַ וְטוֹב לֵב וְכִרְאוֹת הָמָן אֶת־מָרְדֳּכַי
בְּשַׁעַר הַמֶּלֶךְ וְלֹא־קָם וְלֹא־זָע מִמֶּנּוּ וַיִּמָּלֵא הָמָן עַל־מָרְדֳּכַי חֵמָה.
י וַיִּתְאַפַּק הָמָן וַיָּבוֹא אֶל־בֵּיתוֹ וַיִּשְׁלַח וַיָּבֵא אֶת־אֹהֲבָיו וְאֶת־זֶרֶשׁ
אִשְׁתּוֹ. יא וַיְסַפֵּר לָהֶם הָמָן אֶת־כְּבוֹד עָשְׁרוֹ וְרֹב בָּנָיו וְאֵת כָּל־אֲשֶׁר
גִּדְּלוֹ הַמֶּלֶךְ וְאֵת אֲשֶׁר נִשְּׂאוֹ עַל־הַשָּׂרִים וְעַבְדֵי הַמֶּלֶךְ. יב וַיֹּאמֶר
הָמָן אַף לֹא־הֵבִיאָה אֶסְתֵּר הַמַּלְכָּה עִם־הַמֶּלֶךְ אֶל־הַמִּשְׁתֶּה אֲשֶׁר־
עָשָׂתָה כִּי אִם־אוֹתִי וְגַם־לְמָחָר אֲנִי קָרוּא־לָהּ עִם־הַמֶּלֶךְ. יג וְכָל־זֶה
אֵינֶנּוּ שֹׁוֶה לִי בְּכָל־עֵת אֲשֶׁר אֲנִי רֹאֶה אֶת־מָרְדֳּכַי הַיְּהוּדִי יוֹשֵׁב בְּשַׁעַר
הַמֶּלֶךְ. יד וַתֹּאמֶר לוֹ זֶרֶשׁ אִשְׁתּוֹ וְכָל־אֹהֲבָיו יַעֲשׂוּ־עֵץ גָּבֹהַּ חֲמִשִּׁים
אַמָּה וּבַבֹּקֶר אֱמֹר לַמֶּלֶךְ וְיִתְלוּ אֶת־מָרְדֳּכַי עָלָיו וּבֹא־עִם־הַמֶּלֶךְ אֶל־
הַמִּשְׁתֶּה שָׂמֵחַ וַיִּיטַב הַדָּבָר לִפְנֵי הָמָן וַיַּעַשׂ הָעֵץ. [ס]

Chapter 6

1 On that night the king could not sleep and he commanded to bring the book of records of the *Book of Chronicles* and they were read before the king. 2 And it was found written that Mordecai had told of Bigthana and Teresh, two of the king's chamberlains of those that guarded the door, who had sought to lay hands on king Ahasuerus. 3 And the king said: 'What honour and dignity hath been done to Mordecai for this?' Then said the king's servants that ministered unto him: 'There is nothing done for him.' 4 And the king said: 'Who is in the court?'

—Now Haman came to the outer court of the king's house to speak unto the king to hang Mordecai on the gallows that he had prepared for him.—

5 And the king's servants said to him: 'Behold Haman standeth in the court.' And the king said: 'Let him come in.' 6 So Haman came in. And the king said to him: 'What shall be done to the man whom the king delighteth to honour?'

—Now Haman said in his heart: 'Whom would the king delight to honour besides myself?'—

7 And Haman said unto the king: 'For the man whom the king delighteth to honour 8 let be brought royal apparel that the king useth to wear and the horse that the king rideth upon and set a royal crown on his head 9 and let the apparel and the horse be delivered to the hand of one of the king's noblest princes so they may array therewith the man whom the king delighteth to honour and cause him to ride on horseback through the street of the city and proclaim before him: "Thus shall it be done to the man whom the king delighteth to honour."' 10 Then the king said to Haman: 'Hurry and take the apparel and the horse as thou hast said and do even so to Mordecai the Jew that sitteth at the king's gate. Let nothing fail of all that thou hast spoken.' 11 Then Haman took the apparel and the horse and arrayed Mordecai and caused him to ride through the street[s] of the city and proclaimed before him: 'Thus shall it be done unto the man whom the king delighteth to honour.' 12 And Mordecai returned to the king's gate but Haman hurried home, mourning and with his head covered. 13 And Haman told Zeresh his wife and all his friends all that had happened. Then said his wise men and Zeresh his wife unto him: 'If Mordecai before whom thou hast begun to fall be of the seed of the Jews thou shalt not prevail against him but shalt surely fall before him.' 14 While they were yet talking with him the king's eunuchs came and hastened to bring Haman unto the party that Esther had prepared.

Chapter 7

1 So the king and Haman came to party with Esther the queen. 2 And the king said again unto Esther on the second day at the party of wine: 'Whatever thy petition Queen Esther it shall be granted thee and whatever thy request even to the half of the kingdom it shall be performed.'

פֶּרֶק ו

א בַּלַּיְלָה הַהוּא נָדְדָה שְׁנַת הַמֶּלֶךְ וַיֹּאמֶר לְהָבִיא אֶת־סֵפֶר הַזִּכְרֹנוֹת דִּבְרֵי הַיָּמִים וַיִּהְיוּ נִקְרָאִים לִפְנֵי הַמֶּלֶךְ. ב וַיִּמָּצֵא כָתוּב אֲשֶׁר הִגִּיד מָרְדֳּכַי עַל־בִּגְתָנָא וָתֶרֶשׁ שְׁנֵי סָרִיסֵי הַמֶּלֶךְ מִשֹּׁמְרֵי הַסַּף אֲשֶׁר בִּקְשׁוּ לִשְׁלֹחַ יָד בַּמֶּלֶךְ אֲחַשְׁוֵרוֹשׁ. ג וַיֹּאמֶר הַמֶּלֶךְ מַה־נַּעֲשָׂה יְקָר וּגְדוּלָּה לְמָרְדֳּכַי עַל־זֶה וַיֹּאמְרוּ נַעֲרֵי הַמֶּלֶךְ מְשָׁרְתָיו לֹא־נַעֲשָׂה עִמּוֹ דָּבָר.

ד וַיֹּאמֶר הַמֶּלֶךְ מִי בֶחָצֵר

וְהָמָן בָּא לַחֲצַר בֵּית־הַמֶּלֶךְ הַחִיצוֹנָה לֵאמֹר
לַמֶּלֶךְ לִתְלוֹת אֶת־מָרְדֳּכַי עַל־הָעֵץ אֲשֶׁר־הֵכִין לוֹ.

ה וַיֹּאמְרוּ נַעֲרֵי הַמֶּלֶךְ אֵלָיו הִנֵּה הָמָן עֹמֵד בֶּחָצֵר וַיֹּאמֶר הַמֶּלֶךְ יָבוֹא. ו וַיָּבוֹא הָמָן וַיֹּאמֶר לוֹ הַמֶּלֶךְ מַה־לַּעֲשׂוֹת בָּאִישׁ אֲשֶׁר הַמֶּלֶךְ חָפֵץ בִּיקָרוֹ

וַיֹּאמֶר הָמָן בְּלִבּוֹ לְמִי יַחְפֹּץ הַמֶּלֶךְ לַעֲשׂוֹת
יְקָר יוֹתֵר מִמֶּנִּי.

ז וַיֹּאמֶר הָמָן אֶל־הַמֶּלֶךְ אִישׁ אֲשֶׁר הַמֶּלֶךְ חָפֵץ בִּיקָרוֹ. ח יָבִיאוּ לְבוּשׁ מַלְכוּת אֲשֶׁר לָבַשׁ־בּוֹ הַמֶּלֶךְ וְסוּס אֲשֶׁר רָכַב עָלָיו הַמֶּלֶךְ וַאֲשֶׁר נִתַּן כֶּתֶר מַלְכוּת בְּרֹאשׁוֹ. ט וְנָתוֹן הַלְּבוּשׁ וְהַסּוּס עַל־יַד־אִישׁ מִשָּׂרֵי הַמֶּלֶךְ הַפַּרְתְּמִים וְהִלְבִּישׁוּ אֶת־הָאִישׁ אֲשֶׁר הַמֶּלֶךְ חָפֵץ בִּיקָרוֹ וְהִרְכִּיבֻהוּ עַל־הַסּוּס בִּרְחוֹב הָעִיר וְקָרְאוּ לְפָנָיו כָּכָה יֵעָשֶׂה לָאִישׁ אֲשֶׁר הַמֶּלֶךְ חָפֵץ בִּיקָרוֹ.

י וַיֹּאמֶר הַמֶּלֶךְ לְהָמָן מַהֵר קַח אֶת־הַלְּבוּשׁ וְאֶת־הַסּוּס כַּאֲשֶׁר דִּבַּרְתָּ וַעֲשֵׂה־כֵן לְמָרְדֳּכַי הַיְּהוּדִי הַיּוֹשֵׁב בְּשַׁעַר הַמֶּלֶךְ אַל־תַּפֵּל דָּבָר מִכֹּל אֲשֶׁר דִּבַּרְתָּ. יא וַיִּקַּח הָמָן אֶת־הַלְּבוּשׁ וְאֶת־הַסּוּס וַיַּלְבֵּשׁ אֶת־מָרְדֳּכַי וַיַּרְכִּיבֵהוּ בִּרְחוֹב הָעִיר וַיִּקְרָא לְפָנָיו כָּכָה יֵעָשֶׂה לָאִישׁ אֲשֶׁר הַמֶּלֶךְ חָפֵץ בִּיקָרוֹ.

יב וַיָּשָׁב מָרְדֳּכַי אֶל־שַׁעַר הַמֶּלֶךְ; וְהָמָן נִדְחַף אֶל־בֵּיתוֹ אָבֵל וַחֲפוּי רֹאשׁ. יג וַיְסַפֵּר הָמָן לְזֶרֶשׁ אִשְׁתּוֹ וּלְכָל־אֹהֲבָיו אֵת כָּל־אֲשֶׁר קָרָהוּ וַיֹּאמְרוּ לוֹ חֲכָמָיו וְזֶרֶשׁ אִשְׁתּוֹ אִם מִזֶּרַע הַיְּהוּדִים מָרְדֳּכַי אֲשֶׁר הַחִלּוֹתָ לִנְפֹּל לְפָנָיו לֹא־תוּכַל לוֹ כִּי־נָפוֹל תִּפּוֹל לְפָנָיו. יד עוֹדָם מְדַבְּרִים עִמּוֹ וְסָרִיסֵי הַמֶּלֶךְ הִגִּיעוּ וַיַּבְהִלוּ לְהָבִיא אֶת־הָמָן אֶל־הַמִּשְׁתֶּה אֲשֶׁר־עָשְׂתָה אֶסְתֵּר.

פֶּרֶק ז

א וַיָּבֹא הַמֶּלֶךְ וְהָמָן לִשְׁתּוֹת עִם־אֶסְתֵּר הַמַּלְכָּה. ב וַיֹּאמֶר הַמֶּלֶךְ לְאֶסְתֵּר גַּם בַּיּוֹם הַשֵּׁנִי בְּמִשְׁתֵּה הַיַּיִן מַה־שְּׁאֵלָתֵךְ אֶסְתֵּר הַמַּלְכָּה וְתִנָּתֵן לָךְ וּמַה־בַּקָּשָׁתֵךְ עַד־חֲצִי הַמַּלְכוּת וְתֵעָשׂ.

3 Then Queen Esther answered and said: 'If I have found favour in thy sight O king and if it please the king, let my life be given me at my petition, and my people at my request; 4 for we are sold, I and my people, to be destroyed, to be slain and to perish. If we were only to be sold for bondmen and bondwomen, I would have held my peace for the adversary is not worth distressing the king for.' [S]

5 Then spoke King Ahasuerus and said unto Esther the queen: 'Who is he and where is he that durst presume in his heart to do so?' 6 And Esther said: 'An adversary and an enemy: even this wicked Haman.' Then Haman was terrified before the king and the queen. 7 And the king arose in his wrath from the feast of wine and went into the palace garden but Haman remained to beg Esther the queen for his life, for he saw that there was evil determined against him by the king. 8 Then the king returned from the palace garden to the place of the party of wine and Haman was fallen on the couch on which Esther was. Then said the king: 'Will he even assault the queen before me in the house?' As the word went out of the king's mouth they covered Haman's face. 9 Then said Harbonah, one of the chamberlains that were before the king: 'See also the gallows fifty cubits high that Haman made for Mordecai who spoke good for the king standeth in the house of Haman.' And the king said: 'Hang him thereon.' 10 So they hanged Haman on the gallows that he had prepared for Mordecai. Then was the king's wrath assuaged. [S]

Chapter 8

1 On that day did King Ahasuerus give to Esther the Queen the house of Haman, the enemy of the Jews. And Mordecai did attend the king, for Esther had explained what he was unto her. 2 And the king took off his ring which he had taken from Haman and gave it unto Mordecai.

And Esther set Mordecai over the house of Haman. [S]

3 And Esther spoke yet again before the king and fell down at his feet and besought him with tears to put away the mischief of Haman the Agagite and his plan that he had devised against the Jews.

4 Then the king held out to Esther the golden sceptre, so Esther arose and stood before the king. 5 And she said: 'If

| it please the king and if I have found favour in his sight, and | the thing seem right before the king and I be pleasing in his eyes |

be it written to reverse the documents devised by Haman the son of Hammedatha the Agagite that he wrote to destroy the Jews in all the king's provinces

| 6 for how can I endure to see the evil that shall come unto my people?' | or how can I endure to see the destruction of my kindred?' [S] |

7 Then King Ahasuerus said unto Queen Esther and to Mordecai the Jew: 'Behold I have given Esther the house of Haman and him they have hanged upon the gallows because he laid his hand upon the Jews. 8 Write ye also concerning the Jews as it pleaseth you in the king's name and seal it with the king's ring for the writing which is written in the king's name and sealed with the king's ring may no man reverse.' 9 Then were the king's scribes called at that time in the third month which is the month of Sivan on the twenty-third day thereof and it was written according to all that Mordecai commanded

ג וַתַּעַן אֶסְתֵּר הַמַּלְכָּה וַתֹּאמַר אִם־מָצָאתִי חֵן בְּעֵינֶיךָ הַמֶּלֶךְ וְאִם־עַל־הַמֶּלֶךְ טוֹב תִּנָּתֶן־לִי נַפְשִׁי בִּשְׁאֵלָתִי וְעַמִּי בְּבַקָּשָׁתִי. ד כִּי נִמְכַּרְנוּ אֲנִי וְעַמִּי לְהַשְׁמִיד לַהֲרוֹג וּלְאַבֵּד; וְאִלּוּ לַעֲבָדִים וְלִשְׁפָ־ חוֹת נִמְכַּרְנוּ הֶחֱרַשְׁתִּי כִּי אֵין הַצָּר שֹׁוֶה בְּנֵזֶק הַמֶּלֶךְ. [ס]

ה וַיֹּאמֶר הַמֶּלֶךְ אֲחַשְׁוֵרוֹשׁ וַיֹּאמֶר לְאֶסְתֵּר הַמַּלְכָּה מִי הוּא זֶה וְאֵי־זֶה הוּא אֲשֶׁר־מְלָאוֹ לִבּוֹ לַעֲשׂוֹת כֵּן. ו וַתֹּאמֶר אֶסְתֵּר אִישׁ צַר וְאוֹיֵב הָמָן הָרָע הַזֶּה וְהָמָן נִבְעַת מִלִּפְנֵי הַמֶּלֶךְ וְהַמַּלְכָּה. ז וְהַמֶּלֶךְ קָם בַּחֲמָתוֹ מִמִּשְׁתֵּה הַיַּיִן אֶל־גִּנַּת הַבִּיתָן וְהָמָן עָמַד לְבַקֵּשׁ עַל־נַפְשׁוֹ מֵאֶסְתֵּר הַמַּלְכָּה כִּי רָאָה כִּי־כָלְתָה אֵלָיו הָרָעָה מֵאֵת הַמֶּלֶךְ. ח וְהַמֶּלֶךְ שָׁב מִגִּנַּת הַבִּיתָן אֶל־בֵּית מִשְׁתֵּה הַיַּיִן וְהָמָן נֹפֵל עַל־הַמִּטָּה אֲשֶׁר אֶסְתֵּר עָלֶיהָ וַיֹּאמֶר הַמֶּלֶךְ הֲגַם לִכְבּוֹשׁ אֶת־הַמַּלְכָּה עִמִּי בַּבָּיִת הַדָּבָר יָצָא מִפִּי הַמֶּלֶךְ וּפְנֵי הָמָן חָפוּ. ט וַיֹּאמֶר חַרְבוֹנָה אֶחָד מִן־הַסָּרִיסִים לִפְנֵי הַמֶּלֶךְ גַּם הִנֵּה־הָעֵץ אֲשֶׁר־ עָשָׂה הָמָן לְמָרְדֳּכַי אֲשֶׁר דִּבֶּר־טוֹב עַל־הַמֶּלֶךְ עֹמֵד בְּבֵית הָמָן גָּבֹהַּ חֲמִשִּׁים אַמָּה וַיֹּאמֶר הַמֶּלֶךְ תְּלֻהוּ עָלָיו. י וַיִּתְלוּ אֶת־הָמָן עַל־הָעֵץ אֲשֶׁר־הֵכִין לְמָרְדֳּכָי וַחֲמַת הַמֶּלֶךְ שָׁכָכָה. [ס]

פֶּרֶק ח

א בַּיּוֹם הַהוּא נָתַן הַמֶּלֶךְ אֲחַשְׁוֵרוֹשׁ לְאֶסְתֵּר הַמַּלְכָּה אֶת־בֵּית הָמָן צֹרֵר הַיְּהוּדִיִּים (הַיְּהוּדִים) וּמָרְדֳּכַי בָּא לִפְנֵי הַמֶּלֶךְ כִּי־הִגִּידָה אֶסְתֵּר מַה הוּא־לָהּ. ב וַיָּסַר הַמֶּלֶךְ אֶת־טַבַּעְתּוֹ אֲשֶׁר הֶעֱבִיר מֵהָמָן וַיִּתְּנָהּ לְמָרְדֳּכָי

וַתָּשֶׂם אֶסְתֵּר אֶת־מָרְדֳּכַי עַל־בֵּית הָמָן. [ס]

ג וַתּוֹסֶף אֶסְתֵּר וַתְּדַבֵּר לִפְנֵי הַמֶּלֶךְ וַתִּפֹּל לִפְנֵי רַגְלָיו וַתֵּבְךְּ וַתִּתְחַנֶּן־לוֹ לְהַעֲבִיר אֶת־רָעַת הָמָן הָאֲגָגִי וְאֵת מַחֲשַׁבְתּוֹ אֲשֶׁר חָשַׁב עַל־הַיְּהוּדִים. ד וַיּוֹשֶׁט הַמֶּלֶךְ לְאֶסְתֵּר אֵת שַׁרְבִט הַזָּהָב וַתָּקָם אֶסְתֵּר וַתַּעֲמֹד לִפְנֵי הַמֶּלֶךְ. ה וַתֹּאמֶר אִם־ עַל־הַמֶּלֶךְ טוֹב וְאִם־מָצָאתִי חֵן לְפָנָיו וְכָשֵׁר הַדָּבָר לִפְנֵי הַמֶּלֶךְ וְטוֹבָה אֲנִי בְּעֵינָיו יִכָּתֵב לְהָשִׁיב אֶת־הַסְּפָרִים מַחֲשֶׁבֶת הָמָן בֶּן־ הַמְּדָתָא הָאֲגָגִי אֲשֶׁר כָּתַב לְאַבֵּד אֶת־הַיְּהוּדִים אֲשֶׁר בְּכָל־מְדִינוֹת הַמֶּלֶךְ. ו כִּי אֵיכָכָה אוּכַל וְרָאִיתִי בָּרָעָה אֲשֶׁר־ יִמְצָא אֶת־עַמִּי וְאֵיכָכָה אוּכַל וְרָאִיתִי בְּאָבְדַן מוֹלַדְתִּי. [ס]

ז וַיֹּאמֶר הַמֶּלֶךְ אֲחַשְׁוֵרֹשׁ לְאֶסְתֵּר הַמַּלְכָּה וּלְמָרְדֳּכַי הַיְּהוּדִי הִנֵּה בֵית־הָמָן נָתַתִּי לְאֶסְתֵּר וְאֹתוֹ תָּלוּ עַל־הָעֵץ עַל אֲשֶׁר־שָׁלַח יָדוֹ בַּיְּהוּדִיִּים (בַּיְּהוּדִים). ח וְאַתֶּם כִּתְבוּ עַל־הַיְּהוּדִים כַּטּוֹב בְּעֵינֵיכֶם בְּשֵׁם הַמֶּלֶךְ וְחִתְמוּ בְּטַבַּעַת הַמֶּלֶךְ כִּי־כְתָב אֲשֶׁר־נִכְתָּב בְּשֵׁם־הַמֶּלֶךְ וְנַחְתּוֹם בְּטַבַּעַת הַמֶּלֶךְ אֵין לְהָשִׁיב. ט וַיִּקָּרְאוּ סֹפְרֵי־הַמֶּלֶךְ בָּעֵת־הַהִיא בַּחֹדֶשׁ הַשְּׁלִישִׁי הוּא־חֹדֶשׁ סִיוָן בִּשְׁלוֹשָׁה וְעֶשְׂרִים בּוֹ וַיִּכָּתֵב כְּכָל־אֲשֶׁר־צִוָּה מָרְדֳּכַי

| to the Jews and | to the satraps and governors and princes of the provinces which are from India unto Ethiopia a hundred and twenty seven provinces, | unto every province according to the writing thereof and unto every people after their language, and | to the Jews according to their writing, and according to their language. |

10 And they wrote in the name of King Ahasuerus and sealed it with the king's ring

and sent letters by posts on horseback riding on swift steeds used in the king's service bred of the stud 11 that the king had let the Jews that were in every city gather together and stand for their life to destroy, slay and cause to perish all the forces of the people and province that would assault them, their little ones and women, and take the spoil of them for a prey 12 on one day in all the provinces of King Ahasuerus, namely on the thirteenth day of the twelfth month (which is the month Adar).

13 The copy of the writing to be given out for a decree in every province was to be published unto all the peoples and that the Jews should be ready against that day to avenge themselves on their enemies.

14 So the posts that rode upon swift steeds that were used in the king's service went out, hastened and pressed on by the king's commandment, and the decree was given out in Shushan fortress. [S]

15 And Mordecai went forth from the presence of the king in royal apparel of blue and white and with a great crown of gold and with a robe of fine linen and purple, and the city of Shushan shouted and was glad. 16 The Jews had light and gladness and joy and honour. 17 And in every province and in every city whithersoever the king's commandment and his decree came the Jews had gladness and joy, a feast and a festival. And many from among the peoples of the land became Jews

for the fear of the Jews was fallen upon them.

Chapter 9

1 Now in the twelfth month which is the month Adar on the thirteenth day of the same when the king's command and his decree drew near to be carried out

in the day that the enemies of the Jews hoped to have rule over them

whereas it was turned to the contrary that the Jews had rule over them that hated them,

2 the Jews gathered together in their cities throughout all the provinces of King Ahasuerus to lay hand on such as sought their hurt, and no man could withstand them

for the fear of them was fallen upon all the peoples.

3 And all the princes of the provinces and the satraps and the governors and they that did the king's business helped the Jews

for the fear of Mordecai was fallen upon them

4 For Mordecai was great in the king's house and his fame went forth throughout all the provinces.

For the man Mordecai was becoming great.

אֶל הָאֲחַשְׁדַּרְפְּנִים־ וְהַפַּחוֹת וְשָׂרֵי הַמְּדִינוֹת אֲשֶׁר מֵהֹדּוּ וְעַד־כּוּשׁ שֶׁבַע וְעֶשְׂ־רִים וּמֵאָה מְדִינָה מְדִינָה וּמְדִינָה כִּכְתָבָהּ וְעַם וָעָם כִּלְשֹׁנוֹ וְאֶל־הַיְּהוּדִים כִּכְתָבָם וְכִלְשׁוֹנָם.

י וַיִּכְתֹּב בְּשֵׁם הַמֶּלֶךְ אֲחַשְׁוֵרֹשׁ וַיַּחְתֹּם בְּטַבַּעַת הַמֶּלֶךְ

וַיִּשְׁלַח סְפָרִים בְּיַד הָרָצִים בַּסּוּסִים רֹכְבֵי הָרֶכֶשׁ הָאֲחַשְׁתְּרָנִים בְּנֵי הָרַמָּכִים. יא אֲשֶׁר נָתַן הַמֶּלֶךְ לַיְּהוּדִים אֲשֶׁר בְּכָל־עִיר־וָעִיר לְהִ־קָּהֵל וְלַעֲמֹד עַל־נַפְשָׁם לְהַשְׁמִיד וְלַהֲרֹג וּלְאַבֵּד אֶת־כָּל־חֵיל עַם וּמְדִינָה הַצָּרִים אֹתָם טַף וְנָשִׁים וּשְׁלָלָם לָבוֹז. יב בְּיוֹם אֶחָד בְּכָל־מְדִינוֹת הַמֶּלֶךְ אֲחַשְׁוֵרוֹשׁ בִּשְׁלוֹשָׁה עָשָׂר לְחֹדֶשׁ שְׁנֵים־עָשָׂר הוּא־חֹדֶשׁ אֲדָר.

יג פַּתְשֶׁגֶן הַכְּתָב לְהִ־נָּתֵן דָּת בְּכָל־מְדִינָה וּמְדִינָה גָּלוּי לְכָל־הָעַמִּים וְלִהְיוֹת הַיְּהוּדִים (הַיְּהוּדִים) עֲתוּדִים (עֲתִידִים) לַיּוֹם הַזֶּה לְהִנָּקֵם מֵאֹיְבֵיהֶם.

יד הָרָצִים רֹכְבֵי הָרֶכֶשׁ הָאֲחַשְׁתְּרָ־נִים יָצְאוּ מְבֹהָלִים וּדְחוּפִים בִּדְבַר הַמֶּלֶךְ וְהַדָּת נִתְּנָה בְּשׁוּשַׁן הַבִּירָה. [ס]

טו וּמָרְדֳּכַי יָצָא מִלִּפְנֵי הַמֶּלֶךְ בִּלְבוּשׁ מַלְכוּת תְּכֵלֶת וָחוּר וַעֲטֶרֶת זָהָב גְּדוֹלָה וְתַכְרִיךְ בּוּץ וְאַרְגָּמָן וְהָעִיר שׁוּשָׁן צָהֲלָה וְשָׂמֵחָה. טז לַיְּהוּדִים הָיְתָה אוֹרָה וְשִׂמְחָה וְשָׂשֹׂן וִיקָר. יז וּבְכָל־מְדִינָה וּמְדִינָה וּבְכָל־עִיר וָעִיר מְקוֹם אֲשֶׁר דְּבַר־הַמֶּלֶךְ וְדָתוֹ מַגִּיעַ שִׂמְחָה וְשָׂשׂוֹן לַיְּהוּדִים מִשְׁתֶּה וְיוֹם טוֹב וְרַבִּים מֵעַמֵּי הָאָרֶץ מִתְיַהֲדִים

כִּי־נָפַל פַּחַד־הַיְּהוּדִים עֲלֵיהֶם.

פֶּרֶק ט

א וּבִשְׁנֵים עָשָׂר חֹדֶשׁ הוּא־חֹדֶשׁ אֲדָר בִּשְׁלוֹשָׁה עָשָׂר יוֹם בּוֹ אֲשֶׁר הִגִּיעַ דְּבַר־הַמֶּלֶךְ וְדָתוֹ לְהֵעָשׂוֹת

בַּיּוֹם אֲשֶׁר שִׂבְּרוּ אֹיְבֵי הַיְּהוּדִים לִשְׁלוֹט בָּהֶם וְנַהֲפוֹךְ הוּא אֲשֶׁר יִשְׁלְטוּ הַיְּהוּדִים הֵמָּה בְּשֹׂנְאֵיהֶם.

ב נִקְהֲלוּ הַיְּהוּדִים בְּעָרֵיהֶם בְּכָל־מְדִינוֹת הַמֶּלֶךְ אֲחַשְׁוֵרוֹשׁ לִשְׁלֹחַ יָד בִּמְבַקְשֵׁי רָעָתָם וְאִישׁ לֹא־עָמַד לִפְנֵיהֶם

כִּי־נָפַל פַּחְדָּם עַל־כָּל־הָעַמִּים.

ג וְכָל־שָׂרֵי הַמְּדִינוֹת וְהָאֲחַשְׁדַּרְפְּנִים וְהַפַּחוֹת וְעֹשֵׂי הַמְּלָאכָה אֲשֶׁר לַמֶּלֶךְ מְנַשְּׂאִים אֶת־הַיְּהוּדִים

כִּי־נָפַל פַּחַד־מָרְדֳּכַי עֲלֵיהֶם.

ד כִּי־גָדוֹל מָרְדֳּכַי בְּבֵית הַמֶּלֶךְ וְשָׁמְעוֹ הוֹלֵךְ בְּכָל־הַמְּדִינוֹת: כִּי־הָאִישׁ מָרְדֳּכַי הוֹלֵךְ וְגָדוֹל.

5 And the Jews smote all their enemies with the stroke of the sword and with slaughter and destruction and did what they would unto them that hated them. 6 And in Shushan fortress the Jews slew and destroyed five hundred men. [S]

7 And slew Parshandatha [S] and Dalphon [S] and Aspatha [S] 8 and Poratha [S] and Adalia [S] and Aridatha [S] 9 and Parmashta [S] and Arisai [S] and Aridai [S] and Vaizatha, [S] 10 the ten sons of Haman the son of Hammedatha, the Jews' enemy.

11 On that day the number of those slain in Shushan fortress was brought before the king. 12 And the king said unto Queen Esther: 'In Shushan fortress the Jews have slain and destroyed five hundred men:

plus the ten sons of Haman;	what then have they done in the rest of the king's provinces!'

now whatever thy plea it shall be granted thee and whatever thy request further it shall be done.' 13 Then said Esther: 'If the king wilt,

'let the Jews in Shushan do tomorrow also as today's decree'	'also let Haman's ten sons be hanged upon the gallows'
14 and the king ordered it so to be done.	And a decree was given out in Shushan and they hanged Haman's ten sons.
15 And the Jews that were in Shushan gathered also on the fourteenth day of the month of Adar and slew three hundred men in Shushan	16 And the other Jews that were in the king's provinces gathered on the thirteenth day of the month of Adar and stood for their lives and relieved themselves of their enemies and slew of them that hated them seventy-five thousand
but on the spoil they laid not their hand.	*but on the spoil they laid not their hand.*
	17 This was on the thirteenth day of the month Adar, and *they rested on the fourteenth day of the same and made it a day of feasting and joy.*
18 [In summary,] the Jews that were in Shushan gathered on the thirteenth day thereof and on the fourteenth thereof, and *they rested on the fifteenth day of the same and made it a day of feasting and joy.*	19 That is why the Jews of the villages that dwell in the unwalled towns *make the fourteenth day of the month Adar a day of joy and feasting* and a festival and of sending portions one to another.

20 And Mordecai wrote these things and sent letters unto all the Jews in all the provinces of King Ahasuerus both nigh and far 21 to enjoin them to keep the fourteenth day of the month of Adar and the fifteenth day of the same every

34

ה וַיַּכּוּ הַיְּהוּדִים בְּכָל־אֹיְבֵיהֶם מַכַּת־חֶרֶב וְהֶרֶג וְאַבְדָן וַיַּעֲשׂוּ בְשֹׂנְאֵיהֶם
כִּרְצוֹנָם. ו וּבְשׁוּשַׁן הַבִּירָה הָרְגוּ הַיְּהוּדִים וְאַבֵּד חֲמֵשׁ מֵאוֹת אִישׁ. [ס]

ז וְאֵת [ר] פַּרְשַׁנְדָּתָא [ס] וְאֵת [ר] דַּלְפוֹן [ס] וְאֵת [ר] אַסְפָּתָא. [ס]
ח וְאֵת [ר] פּוֹרָתָא [ס] וְאֵת [ר] אֲדַלְיָא [ס] וְאֵת [ר] אֲרִידָתָא. [ס]
ט וְאֵת [ר] פַּרְמַשְׁתָּא [ס] וְאֵת [ר] אֲרִיסַי [ס] וְאֵת [ר] אֲרִדַי [ס] וְאֵת [ר]
וַיְזָתָא. [ס] י עֲשֶׂרֶת בְּנֵי הָמָן בֶּן־הַמְּדָתָא צֹרֵר הַיְּהוּדִים הָרָגוּ.

יא בַּיּוֹם הַהוּא בָּא מִסְפַּר הַהֲרוּגִים בְּשׁוּשַׁן הַבִּירָה לִפְנֵי הַמֶּלֶךְ. יב וַיֹּאמֶר הַמֶּלֶךְ לְאֶסְתֵּר
הַמַּלְכָּה בְּשׁוּשַׁן הַבִּירָה הָרְגוּ הַיְּהוּדִים וְאַבֵּד חֲמֵשׁ מֵאוֹת אִישׁ

| בִּשְׁאָר מְדִינוֹת הַמֶּלֶךְ | וְאֵת עֲשֶׂרֶת בְּנֵי־הָמָן |
| מֶה עָשׂוּ | |

וּמַה־שְּׁאֵלָתֵךְ וְיִנָּתֵן לָךְ וּמַה־בַּקָּשָׁתֵךְ עוֹד וְתֵעָשׂ. יג וַתֹּאמֶר אֶסְתֵּר אִם־עַל־הַמֶּלֶךְ טוֹב

| וְאֵת עֲשֶׂרֶת בְּנֵי־הָמָן יִתְלוּ עַל־הָעֵץ. | יִנָּתֵן גַּם־מָחָר לַיְּהוּדִים אֲשֶׁר בְּשׁוּשָׁן לַעֲשׂוֹת כְּדָת הַיּוֹם |
| וַתִּנָּתֵן דָּת בְּשׁוּשָׁן וְאֵת עֲשֶׂרֶת בְּנֵי־הָמָן תָּלוּ. | יד וַיֹּאמֶר הַמֶּלֶךְ לְהֵעָשׂוֹת כֵּן |

| טז וּשְׁאָר הַיְּהוּדִים אֲשֶׁר בִּמְדִינוֹת הַמֶּלֶךְ נִקְהֲלוּ וְעָמֹד עַל־נַפְשָׁם וְנוֹחַ מֵאֹיְבֵיהֶם וְהָרֹג בְּשֹׂנְאֵיהֶם חֲמִשָּׁה וְשִׁבְעִים אָלֶף | טו וַיִּקָּהֲלוּ הַיְּהוּדִיים (הַיְּהוּדִים) אֲשֶׁר־בְּשׁוּשָׁן גַּם בְּיוֹם אַרְבָּעָה עָשָׂר לְחֹדֶשׁ אֲדָר וַיַּהַרְגוּ בְשׁוּשָׁן שְׁלֹשׁ מֵאוֹת אִישׁ |
| וּבַבִּזָּה לֹא שָׁלְחוּ אֶת־יָדָם. | וּבַבִּזָּה לֹא שָׁלְחוּ אֶת־יָדָם. |

יז בְּיוֹם־שְׁלוֹשָׁה עָשָׂר לְחֹדֶשׁ אֲדָר וְנוֹחַ בְּאַרְבָּעָה
עָשָׂר בּוֹ וְעָשֹׂה אֹתוֹ יוֹם מִשְׁתֶּה וְשִׂמְחָה.

| יט עַל־כֵּן הַיְּהוּדִים הַפְּרוֹזִים (הַפְּרָזִים) הַיֹּשְׁבִים בְּעָרֵי הַפְּרָזוֹת עֹשִׂים אֵת יוֹם אַרְבָּעָה עָשָׂר לְחֹדֶשׁ אֲדָר שִׂמְחָה וּמִשְׁתֶּה וְיוֹם טוֹב וּמִשְׁלֹחַ מָנוֹת אִישׁ לְרֵעֵהוּ. | יח וְהַיְּהוּדִיים (וְהַיְּהוּדִים) אֲשֶׁר־בְּשׁוּשָׁן נִקְהֲלוּ בִּשְׁלוֹשָׁה עָשָׂר בּוֹ וּבְאַרְבָּעָה עָשָׂר בּוֹ וְנוֹחַ בַּחֲמִשָּׁה עָשָׂר בּוֹ וְעָשֹׂה אֹתוֹ יוֹם מִשְׁתֶּה וְשִׂמְחָה. |
| | כ וַיִּכְתֹּב מָרְדֳּכַי אֶת־הַדְּבָרִים הָאֵלֶּה וַיִּשְׁלַח סְפָרִים אֶל־כָּל־הַיְּהוּדִים אֲשֶׁר בְּכָל־מְדִינוֹת הַמֶּלֶךְ אֲחַשְׁוֵרוֹשׁ הַקְּרוֹבִים וְהָרְחוֹקִים. כא לְקַיֵּם עֲלֵיהֶם לִהְיוֹת עֹשִׂים אֵת יוֹם אַרְבָּעָה עָשָׂר |

year, 22 the days wherein the Jews had rest from
their enemies and the month which was turned
unto them from sorrow to joy and from mourning
into a festival, that they should make them days
of feasting and joy and of sending portions
one to another and gifts to the poor. 23 And the
Jews took upon them to do as they had begun
and as Mordecai had written unto them 24 since
Haman the son of Hammedatha the Agagite, the
enemy of all the Jews, had plotted against the
Jews to destroy them and had cast *pur*

—i.e, the *lot*—

to discomfit them and to destroy them.

25 [In summary,] when *she* [i.e. Esther] came
before the king he commanded by letters that
his [i.e. Haman's] wicked plan which he had
devised against the Jews should return upon
his own head and that he and his sons should
be hanged on the gallows.

26 Therefore they called these days Purim
after the name of the *pur*.

And so because of all the words of this letter and
of what they had seen concerning this matter and
what had come unto them 27 the Jews ordained
and took upon them and upon their seed and
upon all who joined themselves unto them so that
it should not fail that they would keep these two
days according to the writing thereof and
according to the appointed time thereof each year
28 and that these days should be remembered
and kept throughout every generation, every
family, every province and every city and that
these days of Purim should not fail from among
the Jews nor the memorial of them perish from
their seed. [S]

29 Then wrote Queen Esther, daughter of Abihail,

(and of Mordecai the Jew)

by all her authority

to confirm this second
letter of Purim

לְחֹדֶשׁ אֲדָר וְאֵת יוֹם־חֲמִשָּׁה עָשָׂר בּוֹ בְּכָל־
שָׁנָה וְשָׁנָה. כב כַּיָּמִים אֲשֶׁר־נָחוּ בָהֶם הַיְּהוּדִים
מֵאֹיְבֵיהֶם וְהַחֹדֶשׁ אֲשֶׁר נֶהְפַּךְ לָהֶם מִיָּגוֹן
לְשִׂמְחָה וּמֵאֵבֶל לְיוֹם טוֹב לַעֲשׂוֹת אוֹתָם יְמֵי
מִשְׁתֶּה וְשִׂמְחָה וּמִשְׁלֹחַ מָנוֹת אִישׁ לְרֵעֵהוּ
וּמַתָּנוֹת לָאֶבְיוֹנִים. כג וְקִבֵּל הַיְּהוּדִים אֵת אֲשֶׁר־
הֵחֵלּוּ לַעֲשׂוֹת וְאֵת אֲשֶׁר־כָּתַב מָרְדֳּכַי אֲלֵיהֶם.
כד כִּי הָמָן בֶּן־הַמְּדָתָא הָאֲגָגִי צֹרֵר כָּל־הַיְּהוּדִים
חָשַׁב עַל־הַיְּהוּדִים לְאַבְּדָם וְהִפִּל פּוּר

| הוּא הַגּוֹרָל

לְהֻמָּם וּלְאַבְּדָם.

כה וּבְבֹאָהּ לִפְנֵי הַמֶּלֶךְ אָמַר עִם־
הַסֵּפֶר יָשׁוּב מַחֲשַׁבְתּוֹ הָרָעָה אֲשֶׁר־
חָשַׁב עַל־הַיְּהוּדִים עַל־רֹאשׁוֹ וְתָלוּ
אֹתוֹ וְאֶת־בָּנָיו עַל־הָעֵץ.

כו עַל־כֵּן קָרְאוּ לַיָּמִים הָאֵלֶּה פוּרִים
עַל־שֵׁם הַפּוּר

עַל־כֵּן עַל־כָּל־דִּבְרֵי הָאִגֶּרֶת הַזֹּאת וּמָה־רָאוּ
עַל־כָּכָה וּמָה הִגִּיעַ אֲלֵיהֶם. כז קִיְּמוּ וְקִבֵּל
(וְקִבְּלוּ) הַיְּהוּדִים עֲלֵיהֶם וְעַל־זַרְעָם וְעַל
כָּל־הַנִּלְוִים עֲלֵיהֶם וְלֹא יַעֲבוֹר לִהְיוֹת עֹשִׂים
אֵת שְׁנֵי הַיָּמִים הָאֵלֶּה כִּכְתָבָם וְכִזְמַנָּם
בְּכָל־שָׁנָה וְשָׁנָה. כח וְהַיָּמִים הָאֵלֶּה נִזְכָּרִים
וְנַעֲשִׂים בְּכָל־דּוֹר וָדוֹר מִשְׁפָּחָה וּמִשְׁפָּ־
חָה מְדִינָה וּמְדִינָה וְעִיר וָעִיר וִימֵי הַפּוּרִים
הָאֵלֶּה לֹא יַעַבְרוּ מִתּוֹךְ הַיְּהוּדִים וְזִכְרָם לֹא־
יָסוּף מִזַּרְעָם. [ס]

כט וַתִּכְתֹּב אֶסְתֵּר הַמַּלְכָּה בַת־אֲבִיחַיִל

וּמָרְדֳּכַי הַיְּהוּדִי

אֶת־כָּל־תֹּקֶף

לְקַיֵּם אֵת אִגֶּרֶת הַפֻּרִים
הַזֹּאת הַשֵּׁנִית

30 And *he sent* letters

unto all the Jews

to the hundred and twenty-seven provinces of the kingdom of Ahasuerus

with words of peace and truth

31 to confirm these days of Purim in their appointed times according as Mordecai the Jew and Queen Esther had enjoined them

as they had ordained for themselves and for their seed the matters of the fastings and their cry
32 and the commandment of Esther confirmed these matters of Purim

and it was written in the book. [S]

Chapter 10

1 And King Ahasuerus laid a tribute upon the land and upon the isles of the sea. 2 And all the acts of his power and his might and the account of the greatness of Mordecai, whom the king promoted, are they not written in the *Book of Chronicles* of the kings of Media and Persia?
3 **For Mordecai the Jew was second unto King Ahasuerus and great to the Jews and accepted by the multitude of his brethren, seeking the good of his people and speaking peace to all his seed**.

אֶל־כָּל־הַיְּהוּדִים אֶל־ | שֶׁבַע וְעֶשְׂרִים וּמֵאָה מְדִינָה מַלְכוּת אֲחַשְׁוֵרוֹשׁ:

דִּבְרֵי שָׁלוֹם וֶאֱמֶת.

לא לְקַיֵּם אֶת־יְמֵי הַפֻּרִים הָאֵלֶּה בִּזְמַנֵּיהֶם כַּאֲשֶׁר קִיַּם עֲלֵיהֶם מָרְדֳּכַי הַיְּהוּדִי וְאֶסְתֵּר הַמַּלְכָּה דִּבְרֵי הַצֹּמוֹת וְזַעֲקָתָם.

וְכַאֲשֶׁר קִיְּמוּ עַל־נַפְשָׁם וְעַל־זַרְעָם
לב וּמַאֲמַר אֶסְתֵּר קִיַּם דִּבְרֵי הַפֻּרִים הָאֵלֶּה

וְנִכְתָּב בַּסֵּפֶר. [ס]

פֶּרֶק י

א וַיָּשֶׂם הַמֶּלֶךְ אחשרש (אֲחַשְׁוֵרֹשׁ) מַס עַל־הָאָרֶץ וְאִיֵּי הַיָּם. ב וְכָל־מַעֲשֵׂה תָקְפּוֹ וּגְבוּרָתוֹ וּפָרָשַׁת גְּדֻלַּת מָרְדֳּכַי אֲשֶׁר גִּדְּלוֹ הַמֶּלֶךְ הֲלוֹא־הֵם כְּתוּבִים עַל־סֵפֶר דִּבְרֵי הַיָּמִים לְמַלְכֵי מָדַי וּפָרָס. ג כִּי מָרְדֳּכַי הַיְּהוּדִי מִשְׁנֶה לַמֶּלֶךְ אֲחַשְׁוֵרוֹשׁ וְגָדוֹל לַיְּהוּדִים וְרָצוּי לְרֹב אֶחָיו דֹּרֵשׁ טוֹב לְעַמּוֹ וְדֹבֵר שָׁלוֹם לְכָל־זַרְעוֹ.

Notes

Chapter 1

1:1–2 Textual problems begin at the very start of the *Book of Esther*. As a single linear narrative, the text offers a clumsy opening that ascribes to Ahasuerus various random attributes. It is more compelling to see the introduction as a compound of two separate and individually more elegant introductions. The first identifies Ahasuerus as an imperial ruler in command of 127 provinces; the second locates him as a local ruler (*melech*/king) based in Shushan. English translations commonly add a bridging word—'that'—to link these two descriptions but there is no such link in the Hebrew. The difference between line 1 and line 2 alerts us at once to two different textual approaches, the associations of which will reverberate throughout the story.

1:2 *Shushan habirah* does not mean Shushan palace but the fortress or fortified distrist of Shushan. The Hebrew word *birah*, from the Akkadian *birtu*, means fortress and, now, by extension, fortified city or just city.

1:3–8 The legend of Esther may be reality or myth or a mixture of the two. In either case, there is no narrative need to recall two parties—one lasting 180 days, the other lasting seven—because only one party triggered the crucial event that follow: the refusal of Vashti to appear when called on by the king. In the standard linar text, Vashti's refusal follows the seven-day party, making the 180-day party a narrative redundancy, and that is unsatisfactory for the reader. A preferable reading is that we have been given two conflicting accounts, as if one followed the other, even though each originally stood on its

own—a conventional way of handling alternative accounts that cannot otherwise be resolved.

1:3–8 There is a difference in authorial tone in the descriptions of the two parties. The first, ascribed here to M, is formal and reflects the king's power but lacks detail. The second, ascribed here to E, is specifically a description of the magnificence of the event. This is a retro-projection of the tone of later M and E texts; at the start of the story, neither Mordecai nor Esther had a presence at court and what is reported must come from other sources or be the product of literary invention. (On the issue of alternative attributions, see the Introduction.) As for the identification of the party in M, there appear to be three different possibilities: reading this passage as a linear text therefore makes no sense.

1:9 Like the duplicate references to Ahasuerus's parties, the reference to Vashti's own party is extraneous and dramatically unnecessary. In the standard text it follows line 8 (E text) but may make more sense following 'And when these days were fulfilled' at the start of the M text in line 5, as here.

1:10 'When the heart of the king …'. Except for the first words 'In the seventh day', this is the first example in the text of a consensual verse, i.e. a verse with no obvious M or E affiliations.

1:11 The usual linear reading of this verse hides a narrative divergence. Ahasuerus's order that Vashti appear at his party has two purposes: (a) to show her wearing the royal crown, and (b) to show off her beauty. These purposes are unconnected and the two phrases have therefore been separated.

1:13–14 The king's question to the wise men who knew astrology (lit. 'the times') is followed by two unusual parentheses. These have been separated according to their apparent E and M characteristics.

1:20 Contemporary commentators who see the *Megillah* as a myth may also regard it as a feminist text. In support of this view is the obviously fantastic idea, contained in this line, that women can be ordered (by men) to honour their husbands. Lines 1:17–18 are likewise treated as indicative of male insecurity and the wish to maintain their unequal prerogative of power. The historic absence of such commentary suggests however that the notion of line 1:20 being satiric is modern; on the other hand, we have too little historic commentary from women to establish this (not that feminist commentary necessarily emanates from women).

1:22 The phrases 'into all the king's provinces' and 'into every province' are duplicates. Attributing the first to M and the second to E (as here) is based solely on an underlying editorial assumption that where there is a choice and no other evidence, the original editors automatically put M before E.

Chapter Two

2:3 Duplication of identities plagues the *Book of Esther*. Here, Hegai is identified as 'the king's chamberlain, keeper of the women' (*s'riys hamelech, shomeir hanoshim*), and again in 2:15 as 'the king's chamberlain, keeper of the women' (but with a hyphen/*maqaf* connecting *s'riys-hamelech*) and simply as 'keeper of the women' in 2:8. See also n.2:8, below. Note also that the Hebrew word for chamberlain—*s'riys*—also means eunuch, as does its Persian equivalent, and many ancient langages conflate the two meanings of eunuch and vizier or senior dignitary. Highly-placed eunuchs were also often of foreign birth or extraction, hence Mordecai's eligibility for this position at the end of the story.

2:5 This line is said out loud when the *Megillah* is read at Purim and therefore appears here in bold. See also 8:16–17 and 10:3.

2:5–6 For uncertainties about who was carried away from Jerusalem, see the Introduction.

2:7 The identification of Esther is beset by textual difficulties. The first of these is the unexplained discrepancy in the name. Here, the first name (Hadassah, Hebrew for 'myrtle' and by extension 'compassion') has been attributed to M on the basis only that it might contain more of a memory of Jewish ancestry. Jewish Bible scholars also like to link 'Esther' etymologically to the Hebrew *l'hustir* (to hide, conceal, mask). The name can however also be regard as a derivative of Ishtar, the Babylonian goddess of love, sex, fertility and war, and has been attributed here to E only because Esther might have been considered, or might have considered herself to be, a neo-Babylonian queen. Of the four statements that follow, the third—referring to Esther's beauty—ought to have nothing to do with Mordecai's adoption of her, unless it contains a veiled suggestion that Mordecai was influenced by her physical attraction and that his behaviour was therefore not exclusively virtuous. Otherwise, this statement ought to follow on from the remarks on Esther's origins rather than interrupting them. As for those other remarks, the first explains Mordecai's relationship to Esther (they were first cousins but he was older) and the fourth is essentially a duplication of the second. Here, the phrase 'for she had neither father nor mother' has been given as an E text because it suggests less self-knowledge whereas 'when her father and mother were dead' suggests slightly more precision and therefore qualifies as an M text. (But see 2:15.)

2:8 Locations within the *Book of Esther* are hard to pinpoint. The text identifies (a) Shushan, which may mean the province or the city, (b) *ha'ir Shushan*, the city of Shushan (8:15), (c) *Shushan habirah*, the fortress or stronghold or castle or fortified district of Shushan (1:2 et seq. but see also n.1:2, above), (d) *beit hanashiym*, the house of women (see 2:3) or harem, (e) *beit hamelech*, the king's house (see 2:8), (f) *biytan hamelech*, the king's palace or residence or quarters (see 1:5), (g) *ginat habiytan*, the garden of the palace (7:7 and 7:8), and *sha'ar hamelech*, the king's gate (2:21). From this it would appear that although the king has absolute rule over the fortified part of Shushan, he has his own private quarters within it, and when concubines are delivered to him, they are chaperoned by the royal chamberlain Hegai who controls the women's house inside the fortress.

2:8–16 The standard linear text is problematic because it suggests that when the other candidates for Vashti's former position were rounded up and housed in the fortress of Shushan, Esther alone was immediately taken to the king's house. This is not possible if, as the text goes on to say, (a) Esther was put into the custody of Hegai who gave her pride of place in the house of women, and (b) Mordecai walked daily to the house of women to check up on her, and (c) she, like the other candidates, spent twelve months preparing for her first encounter with the king. The only obvious solution is to treat the information about her being sent to the king as a characteristically abbreviated M text and everything that follows as a characteristically more detailed and more accurate E text, based on information that Esther (or an Esther) would have known better than Mordecai (or a Mordecai). Separating the text after 'Esther was taken' (*vatilokach Esther*) also solves the problem of the otherwise redundant duplication of 'to the custody of Hegai', as well as resolving the question of who is meant by 'the maiden pleased him' (*hatitav hana'arah v'einav*). As an M text, the him is Ahasuerus; as an E text it is Hegai.

2:10 That Esther did not reveal her origins is also stated at 2:20. There, however, it is accompanied by the comment that she was as obedient to Mordecai when under Hegai's charge as she had been when she was a child. Although this boast could equally be attributed to Mordecai or Esther (see Introduction), it has been given here to M.

2:11 The observation about Mordecai seems out of place in the middle of the description of Esther's preparations, but gives evidence against her having been dlivered at once to Ahasuerus, as stated in 2:8. (See n. 2:8–16, above.)

2:14 Shaashgaz appears to be a junior eunuch, answerable to Hegai.

2:15 Esther's parentage and relationship with Mordecai have already been explained in 2:7 and there is no obvious need for her to be identified again. What the new information adds is the apparent name of her father, Abihail (*Avichayil*), but since this translates to 'my father of valour', it may have been more a daughter's description than a name.

Since 'my father of valour' could not have been used by Mordecai, it is given here as an E text, together with the note about Mordecai that follows. (NB: *chayl*, a variant of *chayil*, means 'army' and appears in 1:3 in *chayil parus oomaduy* (the army of Persia and Media).

2:15 'Everyone who saw Esther adored her.' This is one of numerous sentences that sit awkwardly in the narrative, interrupt it and give the appearance of having been added later.

2:16 The dating of Esther's initiation contains the first reference to a specific month: until now, the only time marker has been to the 180-day party held in the third year of Ahasuerus's reign. There is no need to attribute monthly dating to E except that to do otherwise breaks M's narrative flow (unless it can be said that mensual measure is gendered). The reference is interesting, however, by virtue of its duality. The month is announced first by its ordinal position in the calendar (the tenth month) as it would have been known to the Jewish population—which had not previously had names for all the months and seems only to have adopted Akkadian names when exiled to Babylon—and only afterwards by name (Tevet). This gives strong evidence for the *Book of Esther*'s having been written at a time when Tevet was still a new usage that needed explanation. See also 3:7 (Niysan), 3:13 (Adar), 8:9 (Sivan), 8:12 (Adar), and 9:1 (Adar). References subsequent to 9:1 are exclusively to the name of the month and not its ordinal position.

2:18 There is no evidence here to suggest that Esther's coronation was either immediate or even in Tevet, as some commentators have suggested.

2:19 'And the virgins were gathered again …' seems to be an incomplete fragment.

2:20 'And Mordecai sat in the king's gate …' seems to be an incomplete fragment.

2:19–20: See above. The coupling of two incomplete fragments is one of several examples of bilateralism that has been taken as linear.

2:20 See n.2:10.

2:21 The first we learn about Mordecai is that he walks daily to the court of the king's harem (2:11). We now learn that it was his custom to sit in the king's gate, which is presumably the entrance to the king's private quarters rather than the entrance to the stronghold of Shushan. By tradition, city gates were where the elders of a community would sit, but it is also where beggars gathered and where tax officials were positioned, to extract levies on imports. What the status was of Mordecai or any others who sat in the gateway to the king's compound cannot be known, except that 3:2–3 suggests that it was packed with the king's guards and other retinue.

2:21 The guards Bigthan and Teresh are referred to as eunuchs, as is Hathach in verse 4:5. (See n.2:3.)

2:21 Bigthan appears as Bigthana in the E text at 6:2.

Chapter Three

3:1 No reason is given for Haman's sudden rise to power.

3:4 If it is disadvantagous to be Jewish in the Persian court or more widely (as Mordecai's warning to Esther suggests), it is not clear why Mordecai has declared his Jewish identity. It cannot be that the rise of Haman has made the position of Jews more precarious, or that this is what has prompted Mordecai to swear Esther to secrecy, because Chapter Three is clearly labelled 'After these events'.

3:7 Oddly, the casting of lots was carried out, presumably by Haman's friends, before Haman had yet proposed his idea of genocide to the king. The description of this is dense and unclear: the text explains what the first month was, in which year of the king's reign the casting of lots took place, and what the word *pur* meant, but not how the casting worked. A loose translation has therefore been ventured to try to make sense of it.

3:7 The word *pur* was unknown in Hebrew until the *Book of Esther*. The usual word for 'lot' was *goral*. In Leviticus 16:8 et seq., Aaron is told to cast *goralot* over two goats. In the Book of Jonah, the sailors cast *goralot* to identify who had caused the storm at sea. During the *Kol Nidrei* service on *Yom Kippur*, the

congregation sings to God (in *Ki anu amechah*) 'we are God's inheritance and you are *goraleinu*' (our lot or destiny). The Hebrew *pur* is an adaptation of an Akkadian word (*pūru*) used by the Baylonians, and this further reinforces the *Book of Esther*'s neo-Babylonian character. See also 9:24 and 9:26.

3:7 Regarding the identifying of the month, see n.2:16.

3:10 The repetition (see 3:1) of 'the son of Hammedatha the Agagite' here (and in 8:5, 9:7, 9:24) suggests that 'the son of Hammedatha the Agagite' was a formal title.

3:12 This verse is the first to focus on a particular day: 13 Niysan (formerly Aviv). The new name of the month was given in 3:7.

3:12 The recipients of Haman's command are identified twice: first in terms of
(a) the local officials installed by the king to govern his provinces and (b) the people's own rulers; and then in terms of
(c) the official languages of the provinces and
(d) the local languages as actually spoken.
The difference in tone of the two listings contains built-in assumptions that make one or other list redundant. They are therefore assigned to M and E.

3:13 Regarding the identifying of the month, see n.2:16.

3:13–15 The publication of Haman's decree is described here in three different formulas. Verse 13 and verse 15 both start by saying that the decree was sent by messengers on horseback (i.e. posts). Verse 13 and 14 talk about the decree being published in every province. Apart from these two duplications, verse 13 identifies the victims and the planned date of the massacre. Verse 14 makes clear that the edict is meant to incite the masses and give them time—eleven months—to prepare their attack. Verse 15 adds that the stronghold of Shushan was not exempted, which is significant in the light of the suggestion at the end of the verse that those who lived at the heart of the empire, in the city of Shushan, were not entirely happy with what was being ordered.

Chapter Four

4:1 The Hebrew word *saq* gives us the English word 'sack' or 'sackcloth'.

4:2 For the note about not being able to enter the king's gate dressed in sackcloth, see the Introduction.

4:3 et seq. There is a brief split in the narrative at this point. The first two lines of Chapter Four have concentrated on Mordecai in Shushan; in 4:4 Mordecai's reaction to Haman's decree is reported to Esther by her maidens and chamberlains, and she responds to the embarrassment of discovering that her step-father is wearing inappropriate clothes outside the king's apartments by sending him clean clothes, which he refuses. Esther at this point apparently knows nothing about the decree or the weeping in the provinces, only that her step-father is behaving oddly. Verse 4:3, stuck between 4:2 and 4:4 introduces a different theme. We now learn that all the Jews of the provinces are in turmoil. Esther (having, we must assume, heard about this) asks a servant to go to Mordecai to find out why. From the character of the writing, the rest of this chapter ought to be all E text. It is Hathach, Esther's servant, who acts as go-between, tells Esther what Mordecai has learnt about the forthcoming massacre and hands over Mordecai's written evidence, and everything follows from that. It is not Hathach, however, who reports back to Mordecai Esther's unwillingness to intercede but an unidentified 'they': *vayagidu l'Mordechai et-divrei Esther* ('and *they* told Mordechai Esther's words'). The only 'they' already referred to in this chapter is the maidservants and chamberlains in the M text at 4:4. Had Hathach been reporting back to Mordcai, the Hebrew would have said *yag'ed* in the singular. This requires us to ascribe the text from 4:12 onwards to M; we might even ascribe 4:7–8 to M on the grounds that Mordecai is only talking about himself and Shushan, not about the provinces which is what she asked about in the E text at 4:5. If we do so, however, we cannot explain how Esther has found out about the proclamation or Mordecai's plea that she intercede. For clarity, therefore, we need to return to a consolidated text at 4:6, which deals with information known to both an M and an E narrator, even if the style of the writing from this point argues against our doing so. (The chapter would be a lot easier if 4:3 appeared after 4:4; then the two texts could be treated as linear and sequential, with Esther's inquiry about the distress in the provinces following her response to news of Modercai's personal torment.)

4:6–11 In this account, there is no mention of Mordecai's unusual appearance, as there is in the M text; by contrast, Hathach finds Mordecai in the town square as usual and all seems normal. Whether Mordecai knows what is happening in the provinces is not clear. He does however know about the proclamation posted in Shushan and the threat to the Jews living in the citadel. He gives a full account of this to Hathach, provides written evidence and begs him to beg Esther to beg the king to intervene. She does not regard Mordecai's report as sufficiently urgent, however; she is more concerned with the insecurity of her own position. She fears that the king has not called for her for a month and that her novelty to him may have worn off, and she is aware that to ask for a royal favour without being first invited is punishable by death. So untroubled is she by the condition of her people that she does not even tell Mordecai that she cannot comply with his request: he has to learn this from others.

4:13–14 The first turning point in the *Megillah* occurs when Mordecai spells out to Esther that her present vulnerability is as nothing compared to what is likely to happen at the end of the year, suggesting that her marriage into royalty is perhaps part of the divine plan. His urging comes with a threat, however: if Esther does not act now and someone else does, she will be regarded by that saviour not as part of the Jewish community but as an enemy or traitor, and treated accordingly, i.e., she faces death whatever she does. Given her earlier reluctance, it can be asked whether her change of behaviour follows a change of heart: whether she is now acting primarily in the interests of her people or only of herself; whether she has been radicalised by Mordecai; and whether she is now on a journey —from childhood to adulthood, innocence to understanding, and passivity to leadership. Her initial motives are unclear.

4:15 Only now does Esther accept that her life is forfeit anyway and that she needs to take steps to save her people in order to save herself. From here on, it is Esther who takes over the initiative from Mordecai, who steps back to let the machinery of the court gear up. Having received news that Esther at last has a plan, Mordecai goes off and does everything that Esther has commanded him' (4:17). This reversal of roles eventually, however, leads to a power struggle—gendered and generational—between the two of them, and this is reflected in the text's non-linearity.

4:16 It is not clear from the text whom the three-day fast called by Esther is meant to appease. God is not mentioned. The implication seems to be that the supplicand is Ahasuerus.

Chapter Five

5:1–3 The fifth chapter also begins with what looks like E text, and with events that could only have been known to an E narrator. To ascribe these lines to E, however, removes the narrative bridge linking the end of Chapter Four to the M text at 5:4—the next point of divergence—and must therefore be presented as consolidated text.

5:4–14 There are two responses to the king's question at 5:3, asking what Esther wants. In the M text, at 5:4, Esther asks that the king and Haman immediately attend a banquet—in fact, a drinking party or symposium, in the Greek sense—that she has hastily prepared and where she hopes to put her petition more formally. The king agrees, insists that Haman also hurry to attend, and there asks Esther again what she wants. Her answer is not given until two chapters later, at 7:3–4, where she at last identifies herself as Jewish by telling the king of the threat to her life and to the life of her people. Typically of M, this is a plain, straightforward narrative. By contrast, in the alternative E text, at 5:8, Esther answers the king's question by asking him and Haman to attend a banquet the next day. The delay allows time for two interruptions, both to Haman's considerable disadvantage. The first (5:9–14) tells how Haman returns to his wife and friends, puffed up with pride at the honours that now seem to be racing his way, and of his delight at their suggestion that he ask the king to hang Mordecai so that he can better enjoy Esther's drinking party; the second (6:4–14) deals

with the follow-up to the Bigthan and Teresh story and the sudden and overdue catapaulting of Mordecai to prominence. The two pairs of stories—Haman's rise and fall and Mordecai's eclipsing of him—are the most satisfying moments in the *Megillah*. Told with drama and pathos, and buffed by the irony of Haman's self-preening, they offer the reader the sweetest pleasure: a ringside seat at the defeat of the smug. The E text at 7:2 then brings Esther to the same point of petitioning that was left hanging in the M text at the end of 5:6. In short, each text now refers to two inquiries by the king, one banquet invitation from Esther, and one banquet. This is more plausible than the standard linear text which asks us to accept three inquiries by the king, two invitations and two banquets, all of which recalls the arguably spurious duplication of the king's parties in the first chapter. Duplication is, admittedly, a feature of ancient formal rhetoric, as Esther's speech illustrates, e.g., at 5:7—'my petition and my request' (*sh'eilatiy u'vakashatiy*)—and in her appeal to the king at 8:5–6, but triplication is certainly not.

5:4 and 5:8 Esther's choice of a drinking party rather than a banquet is not so much indicative of her awareness of the king's liking for drink as of the use of wine to formalise and celebrate policy decisions. At 3:15, the king and Haman sit down and drink to confirm their decision to eradicate Jewry from the empire.

5:5 Both the M text here and the E text at 6:10 and 6:14 make a point of the king's hurrying Haman. The implication in all three cases is that Haman is being hurried against his will and otherwise would not exert himself to satisfy the queen's wishes, and this is the first sign of a potential fracture between him and the king. The E text also contrasts this entertainingly with Haman's hurrying home in humiliation (at 6:12).

5:6 For commentary on *v'yinatein* ('[and] it shall be granted'), see n.7:2.

Chapter Six

6:1–14 The whole of this chapter, plus the next two lines, looks like E text. It consists of a night-time interlude, the equivalent of a Shakespearean aside, in which a chance element—the king's sleeplessness—triggers a decisive change of plot direction. Here, the psychology of the king is played off against that of Haman, who badly misreads him. What at 6:6 is clear to the reader, but not to Haman, who has little self-awareness, is that in asking what should be done to the man whom the king delights to honour, Ahasuerus is setting Haman up, but it is unclear why. Mordecai has gone unrewarded after saving the king's life and the king—waking up to a truth, rather as Jonah does *en route* to Tarshish, that a wrong needs putting right—blames Haman; without further textual evidence, however, the subsequent disgracing of Haman seems immense and arbitrary to us. In terms of where the story is heading, it is also premature: the king does not know that Haman has come to ask for Mordecai to be hanged, nor has Esther yet denounced Haman or unveiled Mordecai as her relative and protector. Ahasuerus has therefore not yet had any obvious reason to question the endorsing of Haman's planned genocide. We can only speculate, therefore, on whether readers might once have been able to read into the text some other tension—structural or personal—between the Persian king and his aristocratic Babylonian prime minister (see Introduction) or whether arbitrariness—the same arbitrariness that sees Ahasuerus at a stroke countermand his decree against the Jews—was simply regarded as the privilege of kingship.

6:2 Bigthana. See n.2:1.

Chapter Seven

7:2 The king's E-text inquiry at the end of this line functions in the same way as his M-text inquiry at the end 5:6. Both invite the crucial plea that Esther makes at 7:3, and both are almost identically worded—'Whatever thy petition it shall be granted thee and whatever thy request even to the half of the kingdom it shall be performed'. There are however two differences in the second version: the interpolation of 'Queen Esther' after 'Whatever thy petition' (*mah sh'eilateich*) and the substitution of a feminine verb (*v'tinatein*) for a masculine (*v'yinatein*) in the second 'and it shall be granted'. A feminine verb '*v'teiat*' (and it shall be performed) also follows 'whatever thy request' (*mah bakashateich*). The reason for the feminisation of the verb is unclear. In every previous reference to Esther's request (one in 5:3 and two in 5:6), what is being given is not directly the kingdom (or half the kingdom)—*chatsiy hamalchoot*—which is feminine but the abstraction *mah bakashateich* and *mah sh'eilateich* ('whatever your request' and 'whatever your petition'), and abstractions are by convention masculine. The noun and the verb only correspond, therefore, in 5:3 and in the first case in 5:6, where both are masculine. In the second example in 5:6 and here in 7:2, the verbs are both feminine. Later, in 9:12, *mah sh'eilateich* correctly takes a masculine verb (*v'yinatein*) and *mah bakashateich* wrongly takes a feminine verb (*v'teiat*). It is no solution to say that the verb is responding not to the noun but to what is being referred to—half the kingdom—because then all the masculine verbs are wrong. There are other unexplained gender incongruities in the Bible (*Tanach*) but there seems to be no systematic study of them. The Turkish-born Safed kabbalist Rabbi Moshe Alshich (1508–1593) has suggested that the masculine verb in 5:3 is a reference to Ahasuerus's giving Esther a gift because he is stronger than her, but appears in its feminine form in 7:2 because she is now as strong as him and deserves what she asks for by right, but this only illustrates that commentators have no adequate explanation.

7:3 At the point where Esther finally makes her plea, the text reverts to the consolidated format.

7:4 Esther brilliantly calibrates her plea to Ahasuerus. She makes clear that what she is asking for is that the king guarantee her life and that of her people, rather than merely the conditions of their existence. 'If we were merely to be sold into captivity, I would not have bothered you' is a clever bargaining ploy.

Chapter Eight

8:1 According to this line, it was not until Chapter Seven that Esther finally revealed her relationship with Mordecai.

8:4–6 These three lines seem like an alternative to Esther's simpler and self-sufficient M-text request in 8:3. What 8:4–6 does is to re-state her plea, adding the details of how what she said was worded. As noted in the Introduction, her wording contains two sets of internal duplications, one in line 5, the other in line 6. It is not clear whether these duplications are intentionally poetic and rhetorical, in the style of the *Psalms*, or whether they are themselves duplications or alternative versions retained by the redactor[s]. The novelty that the end of line 5 introduces is that the king's annulment should be published in writing, as the original decree had been, for the avoidance of doubt. Ahasuerus agrees to this in 8:8.

8:9 The record of who should receive copies of the annulment is split into an M text and E text, each of which lists two different or alternative groups of recipients: M places the Jews first; E places them second. As in 3:12, the E text notes that the king's words were translated into the languages of the various provincial recipients.

8:9 Regarding the identifying of the month, see n.2:16.

8:10, 8:14 The mode of delivery of the king's proclamation is duplicated in an M text and an E text.

8:11, 8:13 In addition to the annulment of Haman's decree, the king has now added that the Jews may avenge themselves on their enemies, and the details of this are more extensive in the M text than the E text. Whether the inspiration for this revenge attack is the king's or Esther's or Mordecai's is ambiguous; that it might be theirs rather than his is implied by his invitation in 8:8: 'Write ye also as it pleaseth you'. The plural here (*v'atem kitvoo …*) shows that the invitation was issued to them jointly.

8:12 The M text adds a date for the revenge attack: 13th Adar. Regarding the identifying of the month, see n.2:16.

8:15–16 When the *Megillah* is read at Purim, these lines are spoken (more often shouted) first by the entire congregation and then repeated by the leader. See also 2:5 and 10:3.

8:17 Either this line anticipates the celebrations referred to in Chapter Nine or these are other, preliminary, spontaneous celebrations held in response to the news of the king's new decree.

8:17 'And many from among the peoples of the land became Jews.' Rabbinic Judaism does not hugely welcome converts but this line—which, if the *Megillah* is a comedy, must be one of the most comic—suggests a greater fluidity in pre-rabbinic times. Whether contemporary Judaism would have accepted the prospective converts' motives— self-preservation rather than religious belief—is a real theological question.

8:17 For 'for the fear of the Jews was fallen upon them,' see n.9.2–3.

Chapter Nine

9:1 The two last phrases in 9:1 interrupt the flow of the main sentence, and seem like editorial additions. They function here not as alternates but as call-and-response, the E text giving added nuance to the more declarative M text.

9:1 Regarding the identifying of the month, see n.2:16.

9:2–3: These two lines continue the antiphonal call-and-response structure initiated at the end of 8:17. In each case, the phrases or sentences are terminated or interrupted by a phrase about the people's fear. The lines are different, however. At 8:17, where 'the peoples of the land' has just been invoked, the response is 'for the fear of the Jews was fallen upon them.' At 9:2, where the reference is to 'no man' [literally: 'a man could not …'], the response is 'for the fear of the Jews was fallen upon all the peoples.' These are both given as E texts. Line 9:3, which is about the king's civil service, is given as an M text, not least because what had been fear of the Jews now attaches to Mordecai ('for the fear of Mordecai had fallen upon them').

9:4 Following the reference to Mordecai in 9:3, two explanations are given for why he now commands fear: again, each is significantly nuanced. The M text speaks of Mordecai in terms of a senior figure at the heart of the king's court: a man with a growing imperial reputation; the E text treats him more like a member of the family ('the man Mordecai'): someone one knows too well to be awed by, who happens to be enjoying a lucky break.

9:5 et seq. Difficulties with who did what when start in earnest at 9:5. The king has decreed that the Jews may slaughter their enemies, but on one day only: 13th Adar, the twelfth month. In the standard linear text, unspecified numbers ('all their enemies') are killed in the provinces on that day and 500 are killed in Shushan fortress including Haman's ten sons. At 9:11, the king marvels at what has happened in Shushan and at what may have happened elsewhere in his empire and, apparently tantalised by the killings, tempts Esther to request permission for further bloodshed, which she readily does. She then asks that Haman's sons be killed again, which makes no sense unless she simply wants the bodies hung out for all to see, which is not the obvious reading of the text. (The Hebrew would have explained the purpose if the hanging was not the execution that it seems to be. See Introduction, fn.6.) There follows a sequence of passages that repeat similar phrases but that fit together illogically, interrupt the line or lines of thought, and defy chronology. This incoherence is troubling but can be resolved by unravelling the text into separate threads; indeed, it can only be so resolved.

a) The two conflicting references to Haman's sons need to be apportioned one each to M and E. Thus, according to M, Haman's sons are among those killed on 13 Adar (9:7–10) and it is thus only in the M text that the king refers to their killings (at 9:12). By contrast, the sons are not killed in the E account until Esther specifically asks for this to happen (9:13) and for it to be carried out by royal decree. The significant difference is that in the first case, the sons are killed by the Jews, albeit by permission of the king, whereas in the second case they are executed by the state. That is, what Esther has done is to get the king to acknowledge that Haman has committed a heinous crime against the state for which the sons' killing is elevated to state-sanctioned capital punishment and for which—should there ever be any doubt—the Jews are guiltless.

b) Ascribing to M Esther's plea that the Jews be granted a second day of killing (9:13) solves the problem of achronicity because it limits all reference to the second day of killings to M. Now, E says nothing about a second day; instead Esther asks for the sons to be hanged and then the E text answers the king's question about what might have happened in the provinces. In the linear text, this reads as a rhetorical question ('if the Jews have killed 500 in Shushan fortress plus the ten sons of Haman, what on earth have they done in the rest of my empire?'). Separating the text in 9:12 changes the king's remark from an exclamation of amazement into a simple request for information, which is answered at 9:16: the Jews killed 75,000.

c) Separating the text in this way solves the linear problem of referring to events of 14th Adar before referring to the events in the provinces of 13th Adar. Now, the M text goes on to talk about 14th Adar, following Esther's M text request for an additional day, while the E text merely continues to elaborate what happened on 13th Adar. This is followed immediately, and logically, by the E text note that the provincial Jews carried out their killings on 13th Adar and celebrated on the day after.

d) This sequence—from 9:5 to 9:19—is rounded off by a pair of balancing summaries. M records that the Jews of Shushan killed on 13th and 14th Adar and celebrated on 15th; the E text records that the rural Jews of the provinces did all their killing on 13th Adar and celebrated on 14th Adar.

e) Apportioning the texts associates Mordecai with events inside Shushan fortress and the queen with events in the provinces. Mordecai seems to be interested in affairs of state, Esther with the interests and liberties of her people as a whole.

9:15–16 The repeated phrase 'but on the spoil they laid not their hand' (*oovabizah lo shalchoo et-yadam*) recalls a primary concept of virtue in the Bible. Abraham (*Avram*) in Genesis 14:23 tells the king of Sodom that he has sworn to God 'I will not take a thread nor a shoe-latchet nor aught that is thine, lest thou shouldest say: I have made Abram rich.'

9:17–19 The ends of each sentence introduce another call-and-response chorus: 9:17: 'they rested on the fourteenth day of the same and made it a day of feasting and joy; 9:18: 'they rested on the fifteenth day of the same and made it a day of feasting and joy; 9:19: '[they] make the fourteenth day of the month Adar a day of joy and feasting'. See also n.9:19.

9:19 The E text records that in future years, rural Jews got into the habit of celebrating Purim as a one-day festival on 14 Adar. The M text at 9:23 disagrees. See n.9:20 et seq.

9:20–24 A second division reveals a growing split between Esther and Mordecai. In this five-line M-text passage, Mordecai is seen trying to unify the Jewish people by proposing (9:21) that all Jews celebrate their victory not just on 14th Adar but on 15th Adar. He wants Jews in the provinces and Jews in Shushan to celebrate their own festival and each other's. That they have agreed to do so, and that it was Mordecai who persuaded them, is insisted on by the M text at 9:23. As noted above (n.9:19), however, this is at odds with the E text. The contradiction is best represented as two texts in conflict. Making 9:20–24 follow 9:19 as a single linear text makes no sense.

9:24 The meaning of *pur* has already been explained in 3:7. There seems no obvious reason for the text to repeat it.

9:25 Since the M text has just tried to bring the story of Purim to an end by giving all credit to Mordecai and ignoring Esther, the E text now summarises events by crediting Esther and ignoring Mordecai. In each case, the texts place the stress differently. Mordecai is most concerned that Purim be remembered by a two-day festival that he has or-dained; Esther mainly wants her agency respected.

9:26–28 Since the E text has just ignored Mordecai's insistence on a two-day festival, the M text reiterates it.

9:29–32 The E text here takes over and presents a coda that ascribes all responsibility for the Jews' victory to Esther. The simple E text now identifies her in terms of her birth parentage ('daughter of Abihail'), stresses that it was she who wrote letters to the 127 provinces and deployed all her authority in doing so, notes that the provincial Jews had decided to keep Purim in their own way ('spoke peace and truth … as they had ordained for themselves and for their seed') and grants their independent decision her royal support. This is a radical challenge to Mordecai and one that the M text tries to sabotage. It insists on Mordecai's equality as Esther's parent ('daughter of Abihail *and of Mordecai*') and adds a line to suggest that what Esther was in fact writing to confirm was his second letter insisting on a two-day festival. In the face of Esther's challenge, the M text then repeats (at 9:30) that it was he and not she who wrote to the Jews in the provinces, and co-opts Esther's name to reinforce his claim. This is, in short, a fight for supremacy between Esther and Mordecai and one that the linear text does its best to disguise.

Chapter Ten

10:1–3 This brief closing chapter is entirely M text and gives Mordecai the last word. No mention is made of Esther. It is Mordecai's greatness that is praised; Esther, the eponymous hero of the book, is entirely sidelined. The reason can only be guessed at.